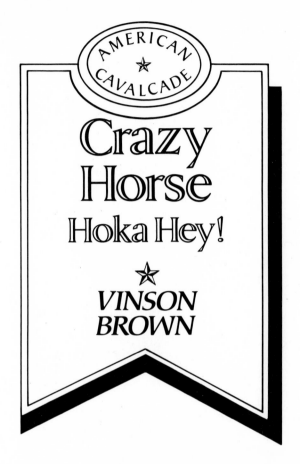

AMERICAN CAVALCADE

Crazy Horse
Hoka Hey!

★

VINSON BROWN

MARSHALL CAVENDISH
CORPORATION

GREY CASTLE PRESS

Published by Grey Castle Press, Lakeville, Connecticut.

Marshall Cavendish Edition, North Bellmore, New York.

Published in large print and condensed by arrangement with Naturegraph Publishers, Inc.

Library of Congress Cataloging-in-Publication Data

Brown, Vinson, 1912–
    Crazy Horse, Hoka Hey / by Vinson Brown.
        p.   cm. — (American cavalcade)
    Reprint. Originally published : Naturegraph, 1971.
        Summary: A biography of the Oglala chief who relentlessly resisted the white man's attempts to take over Indian lands.
    ISBN 1-55905-077-2 (lg. print)
        1. Crazy Horse, ca. 1842–1877—Juvenile literature.   2. Oglala Indians—Biography—Juvenile literature.   [1. Crazy Horse, ca. 1842–1877.   2. Oglala Indians—Biography.
3. Indians of North America—Biography.   4. Large type books.]   I. Title.   II. Series.
[E99.O3C7219 1991]
973.8'2'092—dc20
[B]
[92]
                                            90-48985
                                              CIP
                                              AC

ISBN 1-55905-077-2
    1-55905-100-0 (set)

Photo Credits:

Cover: Courtesy, Naturegraph Publishers, Inc.
North Wind Picture Archives—pgs. 46, 64, 105
The Granger Collection—pgs. 125, 150
Courtesy, Naturegraph Publishers, Inc.—pg. 9
Western History Collections, University of Oklahoma Library—pg. 172

Contents

★

Glossary

(Note: Lakota, in original form, put the main word before the descriptive words. Example: Wichasha Wakan: Man Holy.

Akicita: Persons chosen by Lakota council to make sure warriors worked in a disciplined manner.

Hanblecheyapi: Crying for a vision.

Hoka Hey; Hoye: Cries used in battle.

Hou: Greetings.

Inipi: Sacred purification ceremony.

Itanca: One who has assumed responsibility for his circle of people.

Kola: Friend.

Lakota: "The Friendly People" (of the Seven Council Fires). The Council Fire into which Crazy Horse was born was the Teton. Oglala, meaning "to pour something powdery," was the circle into which Crazy Horse was born.

Matohoshila: Bear Boy.

Minne-wakan: Minne—Water; waken—Spirit or Holy. The Lakota first called the effects of alcohol strange and mysterious, as if holy or spirit. They later saw its bad results.

Paha Mata: Paha—Hill or Butte; Mata—Bear.

Paha Sapa: Paha—Hill; Sapa—Black. The Black Hills were sacred to the Lakota.

Wakan Tanka: Wakan—Holy or Spirit; Tanka—Great.

Wagichun: Wagi—Talking; chun—Tree. The sacred tree of the Lakota is the Cottonwood, or Talking Tree.

Waglukhe: Loafers about the forts.

Wasichus: Whites.

Wichasha Wakan: Wichasha—man; Wakan—Holy or Spirit or Medicine.

Yuipi: Sacred ceremony of healing and guidance.

1

He Who Was of the Old Ones

FROM THE PEAKS OF THE PAHA SAPA, the Sacred Black Hills of the Lakota, the Sioux, the wind sings through the dark needles of the pines, chanting a song about the Strange Man of the Oglala, Crazy Horse, holy man and warrior. It sings of a man big as the sacred circle of the blue sky and the brown earth, bigger than the Oglala, the Hunkpapa, the Brulé, and all the other divisions of the Lakota, bigger than the Wasichus, the white people, who wished his death, big enough to bring a message to awaken all peoples.

It is not without meaning that they carve his feather and his face, his body and his horse, on the great white stone of Paha Sapa, the granite of the hills, heart of the earth, old as time. It is no wonder they shall carve him bigger than the four heads of the presidents at Mount Rushmore, bigger than Washington and Jefferson, Lincoln and

Theodore Roosevelt, the greatest of the Great Fathers who ruled America. Crazy Horse knew a courage as wonderful as the courage of Washington in the dark days of Valley Forge; he knew a message as great as the message of Jefferson in the Declaration of Independence; he knew a wisdom as fine as the wisdom of Lincoln in the Second Inaugural; and he knew also a teaching of the earth and its life greater than that of Theodore Roosevelt, who trumpeted the call for conservation to a sleeping America.

One, two, three, four, almost five centuries of dishonor have come to the red men of America, from the time of Columbus, from the sacking of Tenochtitlan, most beautiful of cities, from the days of the Pilgrim fathers and the padres of California, from the Trail of Tears of the Cherokees, Choctaws, and Creeks, from the defeat of Tecumseh, bitter as ashes, and the broken heart of Chief Joseph, knowing his children were lost and starving. But the days of injustice and misunderstanding must end. Out of suffering beyond suffering the red people shall rise again and it shall be a blessing for a sick world, a world weary of blindness and darkness, selfishness and separations, and longing for the light.

The true wonder and glory of Crazy Horse is not that he possibly killed more of the white

Crazy Horse: "His greatness lay in the purity to which he raised his life, beyond pride and vanity. . . ."

invaders than any other Indian, not that he sometimes stood alone in the councils of the chiefs
speaking for justice, not that no bullet in count-
less battles was capable of hitting him, not that he
was the greatest leader, as some say, in the de-
feats of generals Crook and Custer at the battles
of the Rosebud and the Little Bighorn. These
were all signs of great courage and sensitivity of a
leader, willing to live and die for his people, as
"Itanca" must do. His people take rightful pride
in these parts of his life.

Still these were all as shadows in the firelight,
the dying dust of an old buffalo trail, compared to
his true glory. His greatness lay in the purity to
which he raised his life, beyond pride and vanity,
and his knowledge of the true reality that lies
behind the empty face of human power and
wealth and desire. Out of the Silence he drew his
strength and out of that Silence, in whose harmony he lived, he joins the ranks of the deathless
heroes of history to teach us the meaning of a
greatness all of us need, even more than the
thirsty in the desert are desperate for water.

As a child Crazy Horse sat in the magic circle
of the campfire, seeing strange figures dancing in
the flames and hearing the wind talking among
the leaves of the Wagichun, the sacred cottonwood tree. He loved to hear an old holy man of

his people, a Wichasha Wakan, tell the marvelous story of the White Buffalo Calf Maiden, the Sacred Being, who brought the seven sacred ceremonies and the seven sacred circles of the sacred pipe to the Lakota.

So Crazy Horse knew deeply that story—how two young men went forth to hunt and stood on a high hill watching for game, but saw instead a maiden coming across the plain toward them. When she drew near they saw that she was clothed in handsome buckskin, covered with quilled designs, and that she carried a bundle covered with buckskin under one arm. Now one of them saw that she was very young and very beautiful and his passion was strong with desire for her so that he spoke his thoughts. But the other hunter said, "Put away such bad thoughts, for she is a sacred woman."

Her feet moved like the butterflies as she walked across the grasslands; her hair waved in the breeze like the silk of corn; her eyes glowed as does the sky at sunrise. "Come over to me!" she called to the one whose thoughts were uncontrolled and her voice was as singing waters. "Come!" she called, "and you shall have what you want!"

The one with the immature thoughts ran eagerly and a cloud descended upon him and the sacred maiden so that they were hidden. When the cloud rose, the girl still stood there, but the young and foolish man was only a skeleton lying on the ground being eaten by worms! Then the sacred one told the man whose heart was good and strong to go back to his people and have them prepare a great lodge for her since she would come to give them an important message.

Can you see that boy, who was to be Crazy Horse, listening to that story? In his heart he understood that the maiden was telling him that all women and girls bear within them the great mystery of life's beginning, which the Great Spirit wishes to be nurtured with love inside a family that is filled with love, and not to be touched by the immature of heart who seek only for pleasure. So Crazy Horse saw then that all women were sacred beings and he vowed in his soul that he would be like that good man.

But he listened also to the rest of that story of the White Buffalo Calf Maiden, and how she came to his people, walking in a sacred manner, and told them of the Sacred Circle of their one-ness and love, and how they would smoke the Sacred Pipe she gave to them, and use it in Seven Sacred Ceremonies that would purify them and make them good and honorable to all men and women, protectors of all children, and lovers of the Great Spirit. So the young boy, who was to become Crazy Horse, took these things into his soul until they were like part of his bone and blood. Increasingly Crazy Horse worked to speak the straight tongue that speaks only the truth, knowing that the Great Spirit sees into all hearts and asks of all men the beauty in thoughts and words of crystal clear waters. He grew more and more humble, knowing how little he was and how much he had to learn, feeling the Earth beneath his feet, the Earth Mother, knowing she nurtured all life and was greater than he and yet allowed him to walk on her body. He became one who was too honorable to speak ill of other men; it being more important to see the vision of what they, and the earth, are to become. Even though he sometimes faltered on the trail, as nearly all human beings do, he always returned to the circle. A man need not be perfect to be a great man, but he must learn from all his experiences, good and bad, and develop beyond them through thought, prayer, and action, or his greatness will only be dust upon the wind.

2

He Who Learns Wisdom

THE BOY WHO WAS to become Crazy Horse was first called Curly because of his curling hair of brown, and some Indians foolishly spoke ill of him because he was paler of skin than most of them. But his father was a holy man of the Lakota, a Wichasha Wakan, who had the old and honorable name of Crazy Horse, and his father told him wisely not to worry, that a man stood in the eyes of Wakan Tanka, the Great Spirit, by his goodness of heart, his courage, and his deeds, untouched by the talk of the foolish ones. And Curly remembered this, and, when he became older, judged not all white men by their skin color, but found among them some few who he knew were brave and good and honorable.

When a boy, Crazy Horse learned to leap on the backs of the half-wild horses of the Lakota and tear whooping across the plains. He knew himself to be a member of the Oglala people, though he knew also his blood had in it other divisions of the Lakota, such as the Brulé and Minneconjou, and even some Shyela, as the Lakota called their allies, the Cheyennes.

He practiced with the bow and arrow and hunted with other boys for jackrabbits and prairie dogs and grouse until his shots almost always hit the mark. In youth he grew strong enough to run far on the hills and chase down a wounded antelope or deer as does the great wolf of the plains. And when he killed, he chanted a prayer that the Indians of old always sang over the four-leggeds and the winged ones at death, for they too are part of the Great Circle of Life.

It was Hump, the great warrior and good man, who became the chief teacher or warrior father of young Curly, for each boy of the people must have such a man to follow and learn from. But Curly was lucky above other boys, for Hump had the wisdom of the earth within him and the courage of the grizzly bear and the buffalo bull and the skill in hunting and fighting of one who has long followed the trail of man and animal and learned from everyone a good lesson. Like his father, Curly knew Hump had always used the straight tongue and spoke no evil about other men in the camp, but was silent unless he could say something good.

So Curly went with Hump on the hunting trail and the war trail. He saw this man waste no movement nor any word, but hold the bow or the lance or the gun steady as a rock and strike when the striking counted. He learned from Hump how to lie still for hours, waiting for game, to find the sign of the deer or bear in the slight bending of the grass, to make the clever snares of sedge reed or willow bark for the rabbits and a thousand other tricks of the wild.

But there was pain among the joy in the circle of the Lakota. The horizon was closing in, less land and food, tribes fighting for the little remaining. And so young Curly listened gravely when the tales came of both Brulés and Oglalas down at the traders' stations drinking of the fiery liquid that made men crazy so that some of the young and foolish fought and wounded or killed each other over petty things like a blanket or a beaded bag. And, when he went to the fort of the Wasichus, the white men, at Laramie, he saw with his own eyes the drinking from the dark bottles and the faces turning stupid or wild.

But it was on the outskirts of Fort Laramie, where the drinking and drunkenness had been so bad, that Curly had a strange adventure that helped him later to see with the eyes of the Great Spirit. The Hunkpatila band of the Oglala Lakota, of which Curly and his family were members, had camped for some weeks of trading near the fort to wait for the annual gratuity of blankets and guns and powder that the white men brought from the one they called the Great Father, the President of the United States. Hump, as usual, had growled over this foolishness, which he said was merely a way to lure the people away from the life of goodness and freedom under the Sacred Tree of their religion. But Red Cloud and others of the warriors, including even Conquering Bear, head leader of the Oglala, brought the people here because they said the Lakota had to learn and understand the white man's way. And after all, were not these things given to them as their right because the white men used a road across the Indian country?

One day Curly went off alone to straighten and feather his arrows and to do some thinking and dreaming about a certain Black Buffalo Girl whose face had turned crimson when he looked at her. He was so deep in his dreams that his usual Indian alertness failed him, and he looked up suddenly to see a white-skinned, fair-haired boy standing on a little knoll covered with buffalo grass fifty feet away, watching him intently. In the next second he had an arrow fitted to his bow and the string drawn back, but the white boy, who was about thirteen like himself, raised both hands empty to show he had no weapons, and greeted him in Lakota.

The white boy smiled a good clear smile and spoke again in the language of the people. ''My mother is one of you,'' he said, as if to explain his talking the language.

''But your skin is so white.''

The white boy flushed. ''She is the only mother I know, though I had one long ago who had the same skin color as I have. But because I love so much this mother I have now, I wish to be a Lakota. Can you help me?''

His voice was so sincere that Curly could not help smiling. He beckoned so the white boy came near and sat down beside him. The two looked at each other for a long time without words spoken.

''Wait for me here,'' said Curly at last, ''till the sun is almost setting, and I will bring some things to make you be like an Indian.''

The boy nodded his head and prepared himself silently.

When Curly came back, he brought with him a bowl and some plants that his mother had given him, she who always knew what her son needed, often without even being asked. He started a little fire, got water from a spring, and soon was boiling the plants in it. A while later, when this mixture had cooled into a brown paste, he began rubbing the white boy's skin and hair with it, until they turned a dark brown from the dye, and the fair-skinned boy was no more. Then they looked at each other and laughed a secret laughter that suddenly made everything good between them.

"I will call you by a good name—Matohoshila [Bear Boy]," said Curly. "Come tomorrow, just before the sun rises, and I will take you to my family. We will teach you truly to be a Lakota."

Bear Boy nodded his head in his silent, understanding way, and disappeared over the knoll.

When they met in the morning, Curly taught him the Dawn Song that the Indian sings to the rising sun; the song that tells how the earth and sky are all part of one big circle, with the Great Spirit in the center and man learning to be part of it.

After a bit of practice, the two boys sang the song together, even though usually it is supposed to be sung alone, but the two felt now as if they were one being. And they knew, in the way of all those whose spirits truly touch the wild, that the Silent One was in them and above them and around them.

They went to their horses, sprang onto their backs, and in that same companionable holy silence rode to the tipi of Crazy Horse, the father of Curly. Here, when they smelled the good smell of cooking buffalo meat and greens, they became boys again, eager for the food, and wolfishly chewing it while they grinned at each other happily. Curly's mother and father watched them with pleasure, noting that the new boy thanked them politely for the food and bowed his head in silent prayer before the first bite.

But the reception from Hump was different. He stared at Bear Boy a long time, then reached forward and felt his hair.

"This is a Wasichu," he growled.

"He is my friend!" Curly cried. "He wants to be a Lakota because his foster mother is Lakota and he likes our ways. I have darkened his skin to make him like us, and already he speaks our tongue."

"He is still a Wasichu. You can change the color of the skin, but you cannot change the inside."

Curly's mother stood up. Her eyes spoke to her husband. "May I speak?" they asked him. The father nodded his head and she became straight, like a tall pine, her eyes beginning to mist over with the look of a dreamer.

She said to Hump, ''I have learned much from the far-seeing ones. The white people are outside the Sacred Circle, because they have lost touch with the Great Spirit. They are sick in their hearts and this is why they do so many crazy things, killing without meaning, and using lies when they foolishly think it helps them. They are hurting our people and they will continue to hurt them. But they know nothing of the Sacred Way; even their priests only know it partly, because they blind themselves behind little walls of differences. Yet this will not always be so. They were made by the Great Spirit, just as we were made by Him. They too are part of the circle of life, even though they do not understand. Some day the Great Spirit will bring them into the Sacred Circle, and there are some few already, like this boy, whose eyes are open and who are seeking. I have seen in my dreams the day when there will be a great many like him, and they will come to our people in thousands and thousands asking for help. Our people too, in those days, will be outside the Circle because they will have lost themselves in the storms the white people bring and they will have only the memory of the good days when all of us were under the wings of the Above One. Then our people too will begin to awaken and come into a great circle of unity, gathering their strength like the Thunders coming out of the west. That will be a glorious day."

She sat down and was silent again, her eyes looking to the ground, and the others saw only the good wife, quiet and shy, and they were amazed at what she had spoken.

Hump gave the signal to Curly and Bear Boy and the two youths followed him out to the horses. When they were mounted, he turned to Bear Boy. "The woman may be right," he admitted. "I believe she sees what I cannot see, and I know she walks the sacred way. We will test you to see if you understand and if you too can walk the path where the Thunders lead."

Bear Boy rode erect on his horse like a warrior and was silent, but his eyes eloquently told them he would follow their way.

Two hours later they dismounted on the top of a high butte overlooking the plains below, and Hump led them to the highest rock of all, where they could see the great circle of the horizon on all sides.

"Here is peace," he said, "in the center of the Universe, which is our circle. Remember this peace when you are in battle, when you are hunting, always remember it in times of danger particularly, but in all times. Live up to this peace of the Spirit and do harm to no one without just cause. Be kind to the weak, the children and women, be kind to all men and to all living things, killing only when you need food or clothing, or to protect the weak ones, but killing quickly so you do not cause pain. If you see a girl or a woman alone, do her no harm, nor have any bad thoughts about her, but protect her, for she is a sacred being, and this is the teaching of the Above One. Women are sacred because they are givers of life and their purpose is to raise that life in harmony with all creation in a happy family protected by love where the wife is sensitive to the husband, and both husband and wife are faithful to each other so that no jealousy or quarreling or hidden secrets shall rise in that family, poisoning the air and making the children restless and disturbed and unhappy because there is something wrong between their parents. Out of such sick families come the sick ones who cause trouble between men.

"Sing the songs of the Sacred Circle every day, in the dawn, at midday, and in the nighttime, but other times also, especially when there is a great job to be done or when there is danger, or when you feel wrong toward another person, so that quickly you may feel right. When you sing the songs and are in the circle, you cannot tell a lie

any more than you would take a knife and cut out
your own tongue. You cannot hurt others because
you know the Great Spirit leads you only in the
straight way of kindness and honor. Make this a
habit, day after day without fail all the days of
your life. And do not blame other men or women
and make bad words against them, for none can
judge others, only the Great Spirit who knows all
things and sees into every heart and mind.

"And when you go to choose a wife, do not be
in a hurry, but be patient and watch her for a long
time to make sure she is right for you, and listen
to your elders who may know her, telling the
difference between those who speak about her
with envy or ill feeling from those who speak
about her with wisdom, for the latter will be kind
even though they may warn you and in their
voices you will hear their sincerity. And so test her
loyalty and her love before you marry her, not
afterward when it is too late. Then will the two of
you form a nest, like the nest of the quail, and in
the circle of that nest you will rear beautiful children who call on the Great Spirit by name day
and night and walk the sacred way of goodness to
all men."

Hump had been talking quietly, but now he
turned and looked into the eyes of Bear Boy. He
looked for a long time.

"Do you understand?" he asked at last. When

the boy looked back seriously and nodded his head, Hump reached out his hand and touched the skin over the heart. "It is good," he said. "Here is where the boy decides to be a man, and today I see you have decided. May you always follow the path where the Thunders lead, the straight path and the straight tongue of the Great Spirit."

The boy was silent for a while and so were the other two, looking around the circle of earth and sky, seeing the green grass of the plains in waves stretching to the edge of the earth, and hearing the swallows crying as they circled the bluff, catching insects. Far below a bob-o-link called his crystal song, and they felt the presence of the Silent One.

Then Bear Boy asked: "What more must I do?"

"We will show you many things," said Hump. "How to follow a trail in darkness or in light; how to stand pain without murmuring; how to ride many hours without tiring; how to help others in trouble; how to hunt and how to fight when it is necessary to protect the helpless ones; how to feel and see like a mountain lion, so you sense everything around you, even without hearing or seeing; how to send your spirit out like the eagle when he climbs toward the sun, never pulling it inward in fear or worry.

"When you are trained in all these things, we

will make the Inipi purification ceremony with the sweat bath, and then the Hanblecheyapi ceremony to prepare you for crying for a vision. To a sacred place on the mountain we will send you to seek for a vision.''

And the boy was silent for a while as the wise youth learns to be, thinking of all these things Hump had said. Then he drew himself tall and straight, and said simply: ''I am ready to do what you want.''

Curly and Bear Boy stood together after that in the tests that Hump gave them, trying to run faster and farther, to ride like the wind, to follow the tracks of the animals, to watch in silence from behind a bush or rock the secret ways of the wild, and to harden their muscles in all the ways of the Indian. And so a month passed swiftly, and between the two was a brotherhood that would be remembered always. And then came disaster.

It all happened because of a foolish white man and a foolish cow. The cow, being driven by a white man of one of the wagon trains, had run away from its master, and broke into the Lakota camp, knocking over pots and pans, breaking lodges, raising a rumpus until a young Minneconjou Lakota warrior shot it dead and then butchered it so the meat would pay for all the damage it had done. But the white man went on to the military at Fort Laramie and complained bitterly that the Indians had killed his cow and demanded they be punished. It would have been passed over with little incident, and a horse given the white man to pay for his cow, if he had not kept demanding punishment for the culprit, and if an equally foolish young lieutenant named Grattan had not taken up the cry for punishment and offered to lead a group of soldiers to get the man who killed the cow.

Lieutenant Grattan took thirty soldiers and two wagon guns, whose shots could kill several Indians at once, and went to the Sioux camp to arrest young Straight Foretop, the Minneconjou who had killed the cow. The foolish Grattan, egged on by a still more foolish and partly drunken half-breed interpreter named Wyuse, made such outrageous demands that the Lakota became angry too, and the words turned into the firing of a gun by a soldier so that a great storm broke loose as the warriors came swarming over the river bank, Grattan falling from a bullet from Straight Foretop, and Conquering Bear crashing down with a half-dozen bad wounds, while the rest of the soldiers fought for a few seconds, and then fell under the great wave of furious Indians.

A strange change came to the youth when Curly saw the great chief, Conquering Bear, dying, his body bullet ridden, his head like a skull with the skin yellow and tight over it, and knew that the white men had done this thing because of the quarrel over the foolish cow. Curly felt the loss to his people like a loss to himself, and saw darkly the days of trouble ahead as more and more of the Wasichus came like seeds brought on the wind.

In the days that followed he had to travel with his band, as they left Fort Laramie and headed for wilder country to the north, and, in the rush, he and Bear Boy had time only for a hurried handshake in parting.

Daily he had sung his Dawn Song, and his Song to the Twilight, songs of the Roundness, prayers to the Spirit in the Silence, but now he lifted his voice with new urgency until he felt his soul lifting up to the Great One Above like the sun-flight of Wanbli Galeshka, the Spotted Eagle. Soon something called to him, something asking him to find an answer, to see in vision what he should do. So he rode his horse slowly into the heights until he found a pit left by an old eagle hunter long ago, and here he laid his body down on pebbles of stone and put some between his toes to keep away sleep that he might turn his mind sleepless to the blue sky of day and the star-sparkling sky of night and find a vision.

Three days he stayed in the hills chanting the

ancient chants to the seven directions, crying his desire for help to the One Above. He grew weaker from lack of food and water, fighting to hold his mind from wandering, but seeing no visions.

Twice the sun blazed in the blue sky and passed over to its sleeping place beyond the western hills, and the white stars wheeled twice across the dark blue of space, but still no dream came. At last he staggered to his feet late in the third day and walked weakly down from the hill, hunting for his hobbled horse and finding it finally in a little hollow where he collapsed against a cottonwood, the sacred talking tree, too exhausted to climb on his horse. And here he fell asleep, leaning against that tree.

There his dream came to him like lightning paling the darkness of distant clouds, sometimes in a fog of dimness, sometimes almost as light as day, often filled with whirling shapes and the song of bullets whining in war, and always one who rode and thought and did things with a mind that seemed to be part of Curly. But he woke out of this dream with two men shaking him and fought them wildly until he saw they were his father, Crazy Horse, and Hump, both very angry because they thought a foolish boy had got himself lost in a place where enemy Pawnees or Crows might soon find him. When he tried to tell them he had gone seeking a vision, they were still more angry because he had not taken the purification of the sweat lodge and the sacred pipe rites before going. And then he was very angry himself within, with a deep hurt that he hid behind a face like rock, for did he not know in his heart that he had seen a great vision?

Now in darkness and in light a man may see his future, but when he first sees it and until he understands it and what he should do about it, it hangs over him like a vast cloud and there is fear in that cloud as well as a great calling. And so it was with Curly from that day on until his mind cleared and he knew his destiny. So he became very quiet and withdrawn and went often alone into wild places, until the people called him "strange" and wondered why he did not do the usual things of young men. But they did not know the burden that lay upon him or that he would live one day to be a great light in their darkness!

3

Out of the East Comes Danger

WHEN A BOY HAS DARK THOUGHTS and searchings he turns first to his mother if she is close to him. The one Curly called "Mother" was not his real mother, for she had died long ago when he was too little to remember. But this mother was her sister and also of the Brulés, a sister to the great Brulé Chief Spotted Tail. He looked at her good, calm, strong face and the crinkles of laughter around the clear dark eyes and felt comforted. It was from her that he had learned the meaning of the good Lakota family life.

He could not tell his mother about his vision, for this was to be told only to a holy man, but he could sit quietly by the fire and smell the good smells of buffalo meat grilling or the sweet wild scent of the onions and greens she had picked for supper. And then one evening she spoke to him from a depth of womanly wisdom:

"My son, you are troubled by the white men and what they are doing to our people. I know you see what the Minne-wakan, the alcohol, is doing around the forts and trading posts, and how our young people are too often leaving the Lakota way because of the lure of the white man's pretty things and his power. I know you have been seeking for help from the Great Spirit, and I am proud of your seeking. Let me urge you to continue seeking, but do not get too disturbed by what you find. Remember you are always of the far-vision people and not of those of little vision. There are few like you in this world, but you will live to see even beyond the bad times until the world comes back into the Circle of the Roundness and the Greatness comes again."

"But," the boy asked, "what about the terrible wagon guns of the white men that can destroy many men at a blow; and their faces that I hear swarm to the east of us as numerous as the leaves of the trees?"

"They may cover our country like the grasshoppers," she replied, "and bury our warriors beneath the waving grass and make our people weak and divided in the spirit as they are doing already, but this is only the passing of a long, dark shadow across the sun. The Great Spirit has made the circle of our people and He will make it again, if only a few, or even one, shall keep the dream alive like a hot coal carried from camp to camp for the fire. For one day He who knows all things will spring men and women of honor from the earth, and they shall be heroes spreading the fire into the hearts of all. You and I, my son, will never see that day, but I see that your name will be on their lips when they come and your spirit stand before them in the mountains, for you will have left a trail of light in this darkness and it shall be a guide to our people.''

So the boy—for after all, he was still only a boy—left the fire of his mother with his heart cleared, though his mind still waited for more answers, and he went out into the camp with the other teenagers to race up into the hills on the backs of the wild ponies looking for antelope and buffalo, or to play the war games of pulling each other off the horses at full gallop.

After some months at one Brulé circle, he was riding one day toward another Brulé camp on the Creek of the Blue Waters, coming near after a long day's travel. The Thunders were talking in the west in the dark banks of clouds, and he listened to them always, for he loved the sound. But always the deep voices seemed to be calling, calling, and the clean tang of the air they made and the hint of coming rain made him think of the

Silent One. How beautiful the blue sky was in the east and how bright green the hills of spring, the circle of the earth and sky telling him of the circle which would someday come for all men. And his heart filled with the bigness of all things, so that he hoped deep within that the smallness and the lies and the darkness that the white people seemed to be bringing were only a little thing after all, a winter storm that would die away as storms do in the last days of the Moon of Shedding Hair.

Then his nose caught the smell of smoke and he dug his heels into the sides of the buckskin he was riding, for there was something about that smoke that told him it was not just made by campfires. So it was that he came through a light rain an hour later down to the Creek of the Blue Waters and saw the bodies lying there and the smashed tipis filled with bullet holes. And when he saw this his heart seemed to turn slowly over and over while a coldness descended upon him that he thought would never leave him. Men, women, and children lay everywhere, some of the little ones tossed and slashed on the sharp blades of the bayonettes. His anger gathered like the Thunders within him and he clenched his fists until the knuckles shone white against the brown skin. Now he began to see why his vision showed him riding through hails of bullets, and the dark war cries sounding around him like a thousand hawks shrieking in the sky.

Farther on he heard a soft cry and lifted up part of a pile of buffalo robes to find a mother whom he recognized, Yellow Woman, a visitor from the Shyela (the Cheyennes), hiding with her baby. And he took them with him in sadness and anger back to his people, the Oglala, but remembering that he himself was half Brulé, and that it was the Brulé who had been attacked that day so ruthlessly. He also was part Cheyenne and felt keenly for these people who had visited in the circle of his Brulé relatives and met with disaster.

It was later that he learned how the attack had come in the early dawn, without warning, without meaning except the bitter white army's trick to smash the spirit of the people. And he heard how his uncle, Spotted Tail, had seized a sword from a soldier and cut down thirteen men in battle. But that one brave Brulé, whose deed symbolized those of many others, had not the force of mechanized and hardened professional killers, far away from home and family. He soon learned how Spotted Tail, still wounded from the fight, had given himself up to save his people whose homes were not far away. Spotted Tail had been led away in chains with other chiefs to what many were certain was death. They were being taken as hostages to "white man's land." And now the white man wanted the land of all people. And where would it end? For a while, in the hot rushing of anger, Crazy Horse had forgotten the vision of his mother and forgotten the young white boy who was his blood brother.

4

The Meaning of a Vision

FROM 1855 TO 1858 was the time Young Curly was learning to be a man and warrior. His father and mother and Hump were watching him and sensing his moods and guiding him by a lifted hand here, a quiet word there, a bit of good food, and the warm strength of their presences.

It was a good time, for mostly the white people were far away and the Hunkpatila branch of the Oglala, old Crazy Horse's and Man Afraid's and Hump's band, had decided to leave behind forever the way of the Waglukhe, the loafers about the forts, Lakotas too close to the sweet food, the whisky, and the influence of the white soldiers at Fort Laramie and elsewhere. So they were out in the wild country most of the time where the air was clean, and the plains still likely to be dark with buffalo herds, or amber and white with the forms of antelope flashing over the prairie. How beautiful were the rolling swales in the Moon of Tender Grass and how lush for the ponies and the buffalo in the Moon of Shedding Ponies when the Hunkpatila band of the Oglala prepared for the first great buffalo hunt at the beginning of the Moon of Making Fat.

So the three older ones watched Curly quietly and they saw that he was turning into a man far different from the others.

He did not seem to like to dance or sing or dress himself up in fine skins and feathers and other decorations as the other young men would, especially when courting girls. Always he was quiet and often he liked to go off alone, especially to some lonely hill where the junipers reached out their gnarled forms against the winds of storms. Yet in the semi-war games of the young men, often played on horseback at full gallop and seeking to pull the "enemy" off his horse, he was astonishingly quick, wiry, and muscular so that, despite his boyish slender form, he was able to hold his own with much stronger youths. Always it seemed that a vibrant flame leaped within him, and his younger brother, Little Hawk, followed his every move with adoring eyes.

The old ones noted that he touched the leaves of the blue grass of the plains with fingers that delicately felt every rib; that he would lie still for hours watching the quail leading their young through the brush, or the courtship dance of the prairie chickens when the males flashed and pirouetted and strutted with their great fans of feathers as the females modestly bowed their heads in admiration. They knew he was absorbing the feel of the spirit that lies behind every living thing even as a thirsty child drinks in the cool crystal waters of a spring, and they knew, as the far-seeing ones always know, that one day he would be a holy man of his people.

Around the fire at night they discussed the dreams of the family and the greater dreams and songs of the people, the secret sacred things that few white people ever learn about because they have forgotten the way the Great Spirit whispers in the night wind or the way the world of dreams can lead us on the feet of our breath into new wisdom if we but let it. And because this knowledge can grow only in an atmosphere of faith that is killed by the crush of material things, the shock of too much war, and the queer disease of the white men, called "desire for money," it is very rare today. Crazy Horse and his family, Hump and other pure-hearted ones of the people who came to visit, discussed how already the Waglukhe, the loafers about the forts, had completely forgotten these things and were following the white man's way like buffalo stampeding over a cliff to death on the rocks below.

Curly listened to the talk carefully, drinking it in and thinking about it when he lay on his couch. And he wondered about his dream of battles that someday he must tell to his father or one of the holy ones, and the dream of his mother that one day Wakan Tanka would make the hoop of the people whole again and even bring all the world into the circle.

But Black Buffalo Maiden, the niece of Red Cloud, also occupied his thoughts, especially when he saw her new, graceful ways as she brought water from the creek in the carriers made of buffalo stomachs, or laughing and playing the games of maidens. Once in a while he would catch the flash from her eye as she turned ever so slightly when he sped past her, horse and rider eager to join the hunt.

And at last came the time when he watched her with pride at a feast given by her family to honor her coming of age, and the nights when he stood in line with other young hunters and warriors, and took his turn to put his blanket around her, drawing her and himself into the sacred secret circle that might lead to wifehood and family. The words between them were few, but they were sweet in his heart and mind.

But his father and mother knew the danger in the hand of the niece of Red Cloud. Her parents dreamed of a marriage of power to one who would be rich and bring status, not to the strange son of a poor but honorable medicine man and hunter. So Curly was advised to visit and hunt with his cousins among the Shyelas and to see Yellow Woman again, she whose life he had saved at the Blue Waters. And they hoped secretly in their hearts that he would find a girl there, perhaps the slender younger sister of Yellow Woman.

So Curly went south with some Shyela friends who had been staying among the Oglala, until they reached the Solomon River in what is now northeast Kansas in the Moon of Colored Leaves. Here, in a fine Shyela camp, Yellow Woman hugged him as a mother would and her younger sister looked at him with sky friendliness. Ice, one of the great Cheyenne medicine men, talked to him like a father to a son, about the sacred things.

He played games with the boys and teased the girls with a new sense of freedom, for the girls walked alone here, without women guarding them as among the Lakota; but each wore the sacred rope that was a sign of maidenhood and could not be broken without the man who broke it dying.

So did these people follow the sacred way of the Spirit, taught them long ago by Sweet Medicine, the Holy One, who was to the Cheyennes what the White Buffalo Calf Maiden was to the Teton Lakota.

Now came the time of the short white days in the Moon of Popping Trees and through it and the moons of Frost in the Lodge, the Dark Red Calves, and the Moon of Snow Blindness, Curly played the ice and snow games with the girls and boys of the Cheyennes until he became as expert as they were at the skating and sliding, the running and leaping, the throwing and dodging. And he liked the Cheyenne girls and waited to speak with some of them on the trails to the lodges, but his heart was still far away to the north with Black Buffalo Maiden.

By the Moon of Making Fat in 1857, the Cheyennes were worried again about the white men, and Ice and Dark, the two greatest of their medicine men, prepared a medicine to guard against bullets if their people were attacked. After the first ceremonies, the drums began to beat the solid roaring sound that echoed in the hills and came back in answering thunder. As the beat went on and Curly watched the dancers, the very beat of the universe itself became part of that deep sound. The circle of dancers became part of the circle of earth and sky, sacred with the meaning of spirit from the One Above.

But near the end of the Moon of Cherries Reddening, Curly was to see those same strong warriors he had seen dancing in the sacred way melt before a charge of sabre-wielding white cavalry as the snow melts in the first hot sun of spring. Something went wrong. The warriors went forth without bows or guns because of the ceremonies to stop the bullets, but the soldiers of Colonel Summer used not the bullets but the shining steel of sabres that flashed in the sun and then turned red with blood as the mounted white men drove the Indians from the Solomon River and southward, fleeing in panic. The women abandoned their lodges and buffalo robes to the enemy, weeping when they saw the smoke rise from the fired village.

So again Curly had seen the white men destroy an Indian village with little resistance and he rode back to his people that summer, to the great Council of the Teton Lakota at Bear Butte, with his heart black with anger and sorrow and his mind wondering what his people could do. Still hope rose again when he saw the seven circles of the Teton Lakota, the Oglala, the Brulé, the Minneconjou, the Hunkpapa, the Two Kettles, the Blackfoot, and the Sans Arc, raising their tipis below the sacred mountain, Bear Butte, which rose like a great humped bear against the blue sky. Lakota horses covered the surrounding green waves of the summer plains like clouds of black dots, and the roar of the great drums filled the nights with thunder.

Here he was proud to see all the famous warriors and chiefs gathered. Even his Uncle Spotted Tail of the Brulés stood tall among the others, while still warning of the white men coming like the locusts on the eastern winds. But there were still plenty of the war chiefs also, such as the seven-foot Touch the Clouds, with his famous father, Lone Horn of the North, of the Minneconjous; the Oglalas' own chief, Man Afraid of His Horses and the rising Red Cloud; the withered Four Horns of the Missouri country and his great nephew, Sitting Bull of the Hunkpapas; Crow Feather of the No Bows; and Long Mandan of the Two Kettles.

After the chiefs had pledged their strength to holding the land of the Tetons, and after the buffalo skin tipis had been taken down from around the seven circles, and after the poles of the great central lodge had been stripped and left bare to the winds that would howl out of the west in winter, Curly and his father went alone into the hills to the south of Bear Butte. It was the end of the Moon of Calves Growing Black Hair and the two found companionship in gathering the last of the fall fruits to add to their dried buffalo meat as they traveled. This was a journey together that the father had long planned, a journey to the place of his son's birth, and a part of his own seeing of the future of this strange youth.

So they came to a high place the father selected, a place that looked down into a beautiful vale of Rapid Creek near the place where Curly had been born. The father took out his pipe from the long red-hair fringed carrying case, red-and-blue beaded, and filled with the sacred kinnikin-nik and red willow bark, and smoked it to the seven sacred directions, once each to the west, the north, the east, and the south, once up to Father Sky, once down to Mother Earth, and once to the center of his being, for it is only by merging with all that the smallness of the man can become great.

After the ceremony the father continued to smoke silently, looking down by the creek where the willows flamed in gold, and a doe and her half-grown son came to sip from the shallows.

"My son," said Crazy Horse at last, "you have seen the gathering of the seven sacred circles of our people. It is the last time you and I will see this. There are bad times coming. Our thoughts

Facing the Setting Sun, *by the artist Frederic Remington.
"Our thoughts must rise like the eagles or they will sink into
the dust. . . . A very great vision is needed."*

must rise like the eagles or they will sink into the
dust and be less than the burrowing of the go-
phers. The death of our people is already in our
nostrils like the stink of the place where the vultures come. Our people need leaders capable of
seeing beyond the sky to the One Above and

getting His powers, for whatever is to come to us in darkness, there must still be light to guide us and guard us. A very great vision is needed and the man who has it must follow it even as the eagle seeks the deepest blue of the sky."

He was silent and Curly also was silent, fighting fears that rose within him like dark waves, for was he not only a small man among the warriors, so much smaller than the great chiefs like Touch the Clouds and Spotted Tail? But it was as if the voice of his father continued within him, whispering that a man's size meant nothing in the eyes of the Great Spirit, only the strength of his heart that beat with courage and the will that rose like fire and steel to drive the body wherever it was most needed.

The father saw and understood, and without needing words to tell him, began to build the sacred sweat lodge down by the creek where water could be thrown on red-hot rocks to make the purifying steam. And in that steam later they talked not as father and son, but as a warrior would speak to a holy man, telling truthfully the tale of his vision and seeing even beyond the vision to the reality of all things that are.

So Curly told of how he had seen a man on horseback, a horse that changed its colors through a swirling mist as if it were of many kinds, but which carried that man into dark storms of battle where the passage of bullets and arrows were like trails of fire always, fading, however, before they struck the man. And Curly felt and thought as that man felt, and knew that even as some of his people followed him into those storms of death, others reached out hands to try to hold him back. But there was a light that followed his movements, a light that pulsed and glowed, sometimes almost swallowed by the surrounding darkness, but then blazing up again even as the sun bursts from a cloud. And the man who was to become Crazy Horse had a little round dark sacred stone fastened under one ear, a single feather in his hair, a sparrow hawk flying over his head, his body streaked with lightning and the white marks of hailstones.

The father listened carefully and said at last when the story of the vision was finished: "This is indeed a great vision, and you must do as this man did, leading your people in spite of those who try to hold you back and the fading of the light. No bullet shall strike you from the enemy, for you have a sacred mission.

"Never fear the darkness around you, no matter how great it may become, for it is doomed to pass away and be no more when the meaning of your life and that of all living things becomes clear. Somehow the coming of the white men is not the end of our people as it sometimes seems to us, but the beginning of something bigger than any of us can imagine. But go to the mountaintops, my son, to pray and fast whenever the spirit moves you, for there you are near to the Silent One and He will speak to you when you need help.''

The two also were silent then for a long time and Curly knew that, though there was a great drought ahead, even as melting snow begins its trip to the sea so also from the mountaintops the water of his spirit would someday find its way to the Great Sea.

5

Early War Trails

IN 1858 AND 1859 THE MOONS were busy times for Curly, in his midteens, now, and preparing himself to become a full warrior and going on his first war trails with Hump and other leaders of his people. Remembering his vision he went into battle without fear, but in his first big battle with a group of strange Indians on top of a high hill, he forgot the part of his dream that spoke against taking scalps. He killed two men bravely, but stooped to take their scalps and was shot in the leg by an iron-pointed arrow. He escaped by running down the hill, and when he reached Hump he threw the scalps away. Never again would he claim credit for killing by taking scalps.

At the village they sang of the bravery of the warriors, especially Curly, and his mother was glad to show the two scalps that Hump had saved. But Curly felt very sad over his forgetting to obey his vision until he heard his father walking through the village singing "The Song of a Good Name."

My son has fought a strange people;
  he has been brave in battle.
Now I can give him a new name, the name
  his father bore, and given to many
  fathers before him.
I pass to him a great name.
  He shall be called Crazy Horse.

Soon a great twin line of people, singing and laughing, came to the lodge of the new Crazy Horse. Far into the night they danced the dance of the new name and the new warrior born to the Oglalas, and the new Crazy Horse slept with a different sense of restfulness from having evidence now of what had so long been hidden. His father humbly took the name of Worm.

And not long later, Black Buffalo Maiden had her own ceremony as one become a woman and blessed by the Holy One for wifehood and motherhood. In the Moon of the Dark Red Calves, the old camp crier passed around the village announcing the big event for the pretty niece of Red Cloud. In beautiful white buck-skin, with wing sleeves of blue, her black hair shining smooth and braided, her breast hung with bright beads of many colors, and her face painted vermillion, she sat on a pile of buffalo robes in the open front of her father's lodge. And all came to see her and hear the old village crier sing out the accomplishments and virtues. Yet there were other young men looking at her longingly now, and one was No Water, a young warrior of a family with many horses and honored relatives, upon whom the mother of Black Buffalo Maiden looked with smiling eyes.

As the moons passed, the people saw that although the new Crazy Horse was indeed a great warrior, first in the ranks of the warriors in the fights against the Crows, the horses he brought back were usually given to the poor people, and that he kept only two or three for war. No Water, the brother of Black Twin, and a relative of Old Smoke, had many more horses, and his costumes were always rich with beads, his gun new and of the latest kind. They said he alone of the young men was allowed past the guarding mother at any time to enter the tipi and talk to Black Buffalo Maiden. But Crazy Horse heard also that the girl would not speak to No Water, and he was comforted, sure that she was waiting for him. Yet to claim her he would need to bring many horses for one who was the niece of Red Cloud.

For three, four, five winters now and summers

too, most of the Oglala had been away from the forts, under the good leadership of Man Afraid of His Horses, and others like Hump and Red Cloud, leading the old plains Indian life. It was good to rise in the morning in a free village of the open country full of sacred places known to the generations, and to run down to the nearest stream for a dip and prayer just as the sun rose.

But the news from distant places was not good. For a hundred miles on either side of the holy road, where the Wasichus drove their cattle and wagons across the dusty plains of the Platte, almost all game was now gone. To the east everywhere the buffalo were disappearing, until only their bones lay whitening upon the plains, so that the old men talked of what should be done to save them in the Teton Lakota country. And all knew the Wasichus were coming closer, closer, like a dark sickness rising out of the east.

Young Crazy Horse felt this dark cloud in the back of his mind, but tried to shove it away. Subconsciously he did this, as a man does swimming long in a sea and feeling the tide pulling at him and hoping it will calm. So do the young think for a while more strongly of the bright sun and leaves and a pretty face and forget for a little the great and demanding dreams.

His father and mother watched him and knew what was in his mind, but were patient.

The young man breathed into the nostrils of the horses he captured, the bays, the golden ones, and the others, breathing his spirit into them in the way of old, and rode them until he felt their spirits merging with his. So, in the Moon of Making Fat in 1861, when the white men far to the east were getting ready for the first battle of the Civil War at Bull Run, young Crazy Horse was on a war party against the Snakes or Shoshones, under Washakie, their greatest chief, at a camp on the Sweetwater. The Lakota charged past the camp to the herd of horses beyond and cut out four hundred of the best, whooping them over the ridge toward Lakota country. Then Crazy Horse and seven others stayed behind to fight off the pursuit.

Soon, over the intervening ridges and by a small wood where the Lakota gathered to stand off the pursuit, young Crazy Horse was doing a foolish thing himself, charging on foot across the plain to put out of its misery a horse screaming its death cries in a buffalo wallow and trying to stagger to its feet. Always did he hate to see the weak and helpless in pain, and came when he could to help them. But the old warriors shook their heads over his wild run across that plain, and the fall of the war club that crushed the dying horse's skull to end that keening cry. Again the bullets and arrows were flying around him, but their passage was only shadows that never touched him.

Warriors were rushing to count coup on his running form, but a Shoshone on horseback who was charging the woods did not see him and young Crazy Horse's club swung again, this time to claim a man, and he sprang into that empty but sweat-slippery saddle and was off to his friends before the Snakes could catch him.

So young Crazy Horse came back to the Oglala camp with a new repeating rifle and a beautiful sorrel war horse, but he did not join in the victory dance, nor did he even try to visit Black Buffalo Maiden. He is too shy, his father thought, but his mother shook her head, whispering to herself: "The girl is not for him. The powers have willed it so," but not saying it, for she knew Worm wished his son to find a wife now that he was a renowned warrior.

That winter (early 1862) the trader's sons came in the Moon of the Dark Red Calves and the Moon of the Snow Blindness to trade with the people. They were half-breeds, most of them, their mothers of the Lakota, and some had gone to the white man's school to learn to read. These brought papers printed in the east that told of the great war between the white people of the south and the white people of the north, and of the thousands and thousands of men killed in battle. And these they read to the people. Young Crazy Horse listened and hoped the white people would stay busy with their war and leave the Indians alone, but Worm and Hump said it was really bad because the whites were learning even more about how to kill and one day they would use this knowledge on the Lakota.

Soon a great war party against the Crows was planned, Red Cloud leading, choosing Black Twin and No Water from the Bad Faces. Hump was sent a message to come and bring the two sons of Worm, Crazy Horse and the younger Little Hawk. The older of the two, plain of face, a single feather in his hair, rode his fine red sorrel, won from the Shoshones and now prancing with pride, while Little Hawk climbed on a racing bay, so anxious to go he tore off across the plains ahead of all to show his fine horsemanship.

Even the Bad Faces were glad when the Hunkpatilas arrived with so many good warriors, including also Young Man Afraid, son of Man Afraid, and Lone Bear, the women trilling the victory call as the whole party moved out of the Bad Face Camp, heading west to the land of the Crows. Many men were glad young Crazy Horse was along, for he brought good luck, and they knew he would leave no wounded man behind.

They had hardly started out, however, before No Water complained of a bad toothache, pushing his fist against his cheek and wincing at the pain. They knew No Water's medicine came from the two teeth of a grizzly bear, and that if his own tooth was bad this warned of failure for him coming. So No Water stayed behind while the party went bravely against the Crows.

A week later they struck at dawn a large hunting village of the Crows on the Powder River, and the river mist was filled with racing forms, then the wild cries of the attackers plunging through the tipis, shooting at the rising warriors, and on to capture the horse herd. The Crow warriors coiled and gathered like a wounded rattlesnake, then struck back fiercely to hold off the Lakota while their women and older men got their tipis down and took off to the east. In the running battle of all that day, the Crows were driven eastward still fighting, but their hearts lowered when an old man chief fell, pierced by arrows. Beyond the Tongue and even the Little Bighorn they were driven, but they still fought and protected their weak ones. So that at last Red Cloud shouted, "They have been men! Let them go!" and the Lakota turned back to their own homes. And all remembered how young Crazy Horse and Little Hawk had raced, in the heat of battle, after a wounded Oglala deep among the Crow fighting men, seizing him under the arms when they jumped from their horses, and getting him carefully and tenderly onto the back of the war sorrel, where he could grasp Crazy Horse about the middle and be carried to safety.

Back at the camp of the Bad Faces, Crazy Horse was met by Woman's Dress, a man who had long been jealous of him, and who had been called as a boy "The Pretty One." Woman's Dress's dark eyes gleamed triumphantly as he reported, "My cousin, No Water, is walking under the blanket with one whom you know."

Young Crazy Horse knew this meant that Black Buffalo Maiden was now Black Buffalo Woman and married. He stopped his horse and stood perfectly still as if struck by sky fire, his face turning pale as the moonbeams. If his hand had not been nerveless with shock, he would have drawn his knife and driven it swift as an arrow into the heart of Woman's Dress. But when he recovered, the man was gone, a malicious shadow, and the young warrior drooped like a winter-struck sunflower as he turned his horse sadly for home without a word.

Worm and his mother saw him coming from afar at the Hunkpatila Camp, and the two knew instantly what had happened. No word was said as they opened the flap for him into the tipi, but they saw him fling himself down on his bed and lie as if dead. Gently the father walked silently and sadly away with his wife to the tipi of High Horse, his brother. There they would stay until the young man was ready to face the world again.

In three days' time, young Crazy Horse noticed that his father had covered brush over the door of the tipi to guard his son from prying eyes and disturbance, and he wept a little in gratitude. Then he shook himself like a great bear after battle, put powder and bullets into a sack for war, got on his red sorrel, lifted the noble head high, and pointed the flaming nostrils toward the east and north once more against the Crows.

After that trip he became part of the camp again, a little more kind if possible than before to find a widow or an old man in need of meat or a horse, a little more silent as he listened around the campfire to the stories and legends. Some of the mothers with marriageable girls hoped he would be visiting their lodges, but he kept to himself and they could see he was thinking long thoughts, though not about their daughters.

For months No Water and Black Buffalo Woman stayed far away from the Hunkpatila camp, but one evening in the Moon of Colored Leaves, when the cirrus clouds were feathering their arrows across the western sky, Crazy Horse came riding by the camp of the Bad Faces and suddenly saw the young wife of No Water rising from behind a nearby clump of the fragrant sage bushes where she had been gathering potherbs. At first she threw her blanket over her startled face, but, when no harsh words sounded, she dropped it slowly and spoke softly:

"My father and my mother and my brothers said I had a duty—and you remember what the old wise one said about the duty of the daughter . . ." Her voice trailed away into the stillness.

The young man raised his hand. *"Hou, Kola!"* he replied. "Let there be no bad words between us. I am no longer angry. You have chosen!" And he rode away into a growing silence, until the young woman took her basket suddenly and threw it with all its herbs as far as she could, then turned her head and wept.

their skins. There are too many now among the Lakota who are following the white man's way of quarreling and drinking rather than the way of the Hanblecheyapi. But this young man is leaving the white man's way to become like us, a part of the circle. In the circle, all are brothers, regardless of the color of their skins.''

And Little Big Man, short but chunky and strong as his name meant, sulked off by himself, his eyes growing dark as they followed the movements of Bear Boy.

Bear Boy was silent, but he stood straight and proud, with his hands turned outward and his face to the sun. There was no need for him to talk, for they knew what he meant. So they took him into their lodges and laughed with him and gave him of the meat of the chase, roasted over the coals until the fine smell of buffalo tongues and elk steaks rose in the warm air of spring. The young white man was one with them, as in the past when young Curly had found him among the sand hills near Fort Laramie and painted his face and hair brown to make him look Lakota.

Soon it was the Moon of Making Fat, and young Casper Collins joined Bear Boy, Crazy Horse, and the Hunkpatila on a buffalo hunt. The hunters moved out in the good way of old over the plains near the Powder River, with the Akicita

A woodcut, made in the 1850s, depicting Sioux Indians. "Up and over the hills the Lakota hunters race on their horses, a wild keening coming from their lips. . . ."

holding back the eager young men so the scouts, such as Crazy Horse and Hump, could give the signal for when the charge could be made. They saw in time, the herd, like black clumps on the rolling hills, near the river and gave the signal for the surround. At this, the hunters got off and led their horses slowly up to the ridge crests, then waved the blanket again for the charge, when every man was in his proper place.

Up and over the hills the Lakota hunters raced on their horses, a wild keening coming from their lips when the herd was struck. The herd plunged away, the horses with men on their backs running among them, the dust clouds darkening the sun, and the smell of blood and sweat in the air. Bellowing filled the sky also and the wild shouting, the day great for a hunt, and the Akicita making sure any wounded buffalo was killed and not allowed to wander in pain; for the Indian knows the buffalo is his brother, even though he must kill him for food, clothing, and shelter.

Casper Collins and Bear Boy each had a bull down, with a bullet apiece, the red gore darkening the grass and the knives out for the skinning. Like the Lakota, they knew that each bit of animal that could be used must be saved, meat and even the intestines for the meals of the future, some eaten right away and some smoked and dried into jerky for the coming winter. The stomach made a fine waterproof bag for carrying water; the sinews from the backbone made thread for the women and bow-strings and bow-backing for the hunters; the bones could be made into tools and awls when the white man's steel was not available; the horns were used in the dances or for tools; the hoofs made a glue; the skins made tents, blankets, and robes; and even the tail could be used for a fly switch or sweeping out a tipi.

As Bear Boy bent over to start cutting away the skin, he heard a swish like a little sudden wind, and looked up to see an arrow sticking in the ground beside him. It had flown by where his upper body had been only a second before. When Crazy Horse came running up, Bear Boy pointed to the arrow, then to his body and lifted up to show where the arrow might have gone. Crazy Horse's eyes narrowed.

"Let us hope," he said, "that this was only an accident. But be on guard, my friend."

After the last meat of the hunt had been dried, the people had a time for leisure, and it was then that Worm prepared the Inipi and Hanblecheyapi ceremonies for Bear Boy. Worm explained them: "In the long ago seven ceremonies for the seven sacred circles were given to us, some by White Buffalo Calf Maiden, and some by Holy Ones long before her. By these ceremonies our people have life. Forgetting them, as is done by the Loafers about the Forts, means death for our sacred tree and sacred hoop and for our people. Each ceremony has special songs that go with it. All these ceremonies and songs come from the Great One Above. Your people also probably have sacred songs and ceremonies, but either they have forgotten how to use them, or they have lost their power because of the way the religion of the Wasichus is divided into little parts, each going a different way. Long ago our old ones told us that they knew a strange people would come out of the east and they might destroy our songs for a while, but that one day they would come back and instead of seven circles there would be nine. What this means I do not know. All I can do now is to teach you the meaning of these things so you will see why they are important to us and to the Great Spirit.

"Listen carefully. These two ceremonies, the Inipi and the Hanblecheyapi, are probably the most important of the seven; in fact we use parts of all the seven in these two so that when we only have time for two they contain the meaning and feeling of all. The Inipi ceremony is the purification ceremony to make you ready so you can go up on the mountain for the Hanblecheyapi. Sometimes when we talk to our young men and women about purification, they listen only with one ear, or none at all. This did not use to be, but has been happening since the coming of the Wasichus.

"When you go up on the mountain to cry for a vision, the Hanblecheyapi, you must go completely purified by the Inipi ceremony, so that the whole time you are on that mountain, having no food and maybe no water if the days are not too hot and dry, you will be sending out your spirit into the sky and down to the earth and out to the four directions like a great river flowing down from the hills, never stopping. And so your spirit will come into contact with the Great Spirit and He will speak to you through the birds or animals, or the clouds or the thunder, or the wind in the leaves of the trees, until you see or hear something that opens the way for you into the heart of the universe and you will become one with all things that live.

"Remember that there is a falling away from this searching among our young people. I am hoping that you who are of the Wasichus, but who also want to be one with us, will be of help someday in turning our people back to the search for the Great Spirit that they need so badly, and your people also."

Crazy Horse and Worm were proud to see that Bear Boy listened with all his heart and that when he prepared for the Inipi ceremony he did all that he was told to do without a murmur. Worm was first in the sweat lodge to make the opening prayer, while young Crazy Horse, learning the way of the holy men, made the sacred fire at the end of the trench that faced the east. Here the hot rocks were prepared and later brought into the lodge after all had filed within, so that the water of life could be thrown upon them, along with the sacred sweet grass and sage to bring forth the fragrant steam. Four times the sweat lodge was made dark and four times it was opened up to light, to signify the four ages of the earth and the battle between light and darkness. Four times the water and the sage and sweet grass were thrown on the red-hot rocks to purify the bodies of those within the lodge and cleanse their minds also of all but spiritual things.

Carrying a buffalo robe and naked except for a loin cloth, Bear Boy left the Inipi ceremony for a nearby butte, riding a horse led by young Crazy Horse and followed by Worm. At the base of the butte they made the ceremony to the seven directions, smoking the sacred pipe, and Worm called on the powers of the Universe to help the young man who came crying for a vision. Thus was the Hanblecheyapi for Bear Boy begun, and he walked to the top of the butte where a place was prepared for him with a bed made of sagebrush, and a circle of the sacred tobacco, plus a small offering of dried meat and wild fruits to the Powers. Also five poles were put up, including a center pole and four poles for the four winds, each with a cloth, one red, one black, one white, and one yellow. Here he was told to circle to the directions, holding his pipe with the stem outward, pointing first to the west, then the north, east, and south, twice up to Father Sky, and once down to Mother Earth, making seven prayers or songs as he did so.

"Be of strong heart," said Worm as he left him, "and may your heart reach the Great Spirit because it is pure and good. Pray that you may have a vision of how to help your people and mine. When you have had a vision and wish to come down, lower the central pole and we will come for you. Otherwise we will come for you at the end of the fourth day."

The days passed and the pole was not lowered, but on the third evening a great dark cloud came out of the west full of the yellow streaks of lightning and loud with the roar of the Thunder Beings.

"This is a test," said Worm, "whether he will be strong. We will know when we see him whether his power was great, because there will be no sign of rain where he stands, though we can see now that it is pouring up there on the mountain."

On the fourth day they saw that all the poles were down, so they climbed up the rocks and came to where Bear Boy had been, but there was no sign of him, though all around the sacred place where he had been praying there was much sign of rain, but none where he had stood. They followed his tracks down the mountainside and found him sprawled on a large rock with a gash on his head where he had fallen in the darkness and been knocked unconscious. When his face was washed with water, the wound dressed, and a damp skin pressed to his lips, he came out of his deep sleep, muttering for a while as if he had lost his mind, but gradually his eyes cleared and he began to look at them intelligently, though his eyes were dark with something they could not understand.

They put him on a horse and brought him down to the camp, where the mother of young Crazy Horse put a soothing compact of wet medicinal leaves on his head, and, at last, he spoke.

"When the thunder and lightning came, I was afraid at first," he said, "but then I remembered that the spirit that is strong needs to fear nothing, and I prayed harder. Then I saw the hail falling near me, but none of it struck me, and I felt very strong, for I knew the Spirit was protecting me. I lay down while the Thunders were talking above me, and suddenly I was asleep. In my dream I saw a man lying on a rock with an arrow in his back, but not where the heart is, and I saw that he was alive and that he was me, but I knew he was dying and I felt very sad.

"Then, in another place, as if my eyes could see close up of something faraway, I saw another man lying with a wound in his back just as my wound had been, but without an arrow in it. He was an Indian, and he also was dying, but I could not see who he was. But around him I heard a great wailing.

''The wailing did not die for a long time. When it did, I was back with the man who was me lying near death. Below him was a canyon where a great river of people were walking, white people, with their faces turned toward the west, but they seemed not to be human beings, but all with their eyes fixed on something in the distance that held them like a magnet. Yet, now and then, one or two or three would pull their glances away from this thing and leave the great stream and start to try to climb out of the canyon to where the man who was me was lying.

''And that is all I knew until you woke me up and I found this wound in my head.''

Young Crazy Horse and his father were silent for a very long time, and Bear Boy looked from one to the other in a strange way until at last Worm spoke.

''The Thunders gave you a sight into the future. You are to die, probably in battle, but you are also to live in the minds of men who will hear of your dream and listen. These are those who climb the cliffs of the spirit away from the white man's way that is destroying the earth, as we were told it would, long ago, by our great holy man, Drinks Water. You have sought the good Lakota spirit way of going to the mountain to pray and fast, and one day others like you of your people will seek that way too, but it is too early yet for that beginning. You and the Indian you saw in your vision, who also was wounded and dying, will die in the dark time, when many are forgetting the spirit, but both of you will help your people into a new day of light and harmony. Would that we all might live to see that day when your people and my people will come back to greatness! And it is good to know that in that time my people will help yours.''

It seemed in the next month bad news followed on bad news. First came the Santee Sioux, drifting out of Minnesota with their tale of the bloody fight against the whites in 1862, when no food had been given to the Indians and they rose in frenzy. Then the peaceful Yankton Sioux were attacked because of what the Santee had done, and Crazy Horse knew more women and children must have suffered.

He heard how the soldiers were swarming now on the Holy Road and how a new breed of soldiers had come, men who were close to the Gray Men, the thieves and cutthroats of the West, in their idea that Indians were little more than lice to be ground beneath their boots. He saw Little Hawk happily sharpening his hunting knife and war hatchet, and singing a song about blood soon to be let, but Crazy Horse remembered the day at the Blue Water when he had seen the cut-up bodies of women and children, and he could not be happy at the prospect of war.

Then worst of all in the ice-cold Moon of Popping Trees, 1864, came the news of the massacre of Black Kettle's Cheyennes, over four hundred of them and mostly women and children, at Sand Creek on the Big Bend of the Arkansas River, by Colonel Chivington of the Colorado Volunteers. That these peaceful Cheyennes, under a peace chief, Black Kettle, could be so easily killed when they were supposed to be under the protection of the white government sent the pipe of war from tribe to tribe like a great wind.

Two days before the news of the massacre came to the camp of the Hunkpatila, Bear Boy had left the Oglalas to rejoin his parents at Fort Laramie. Now Crazy Horse left the camp to follow his trail, fearful that the young white man would be attacked before he knew what had happened far to the south. Though Crazy Horse raced his best horse to catch up with Bear Boy it was not until three days passed that he found him. Ah, indeed, it was too late, as the vision had spoken truly. Far off he saw the figure lying on the rock, and when he got close, there was the arrow in the back. A cry of rage rose in his throat, but there was no one near to vent his anger on, only the weak winter sun in the sky, and the blood congealing into ice on the rock. The young white man was not yet dead, but the birds of death were hovering close.

Crazy Horse knew it was useless and too painful to pull out the arrow. He took off his buffalo robe from his horse and spread it around the still figure, putting a bunched piece of cloth under his head for a pillow, and put his head low. The voice came so weakly that he could hardly hear it.

"My vision came true!" There was a hint of triumph through the pain, and even a little laughter. How could a man die so bravely, and such a good man? "It is Crazy Horse who has come, I know, my friend! My friend! If my death would only help you and your people, but I know that a longer darkness must come first before the light. Remember me when you too die, and do not curse my people. Remember that I love you, and one day there will be many of my skin who will love you too. For at last they shall understand that we are all men of the same blood and the Great Spirit is our Maker!"

The last word was only a whisper, barely understood, and then there was no more. When Crazy Horse felt the body stiffen his throat broke loose with a great sob and he flung himself beside his dead friend.

7

Little Wars and Bad Luck

THERE WAS WAR WITH THE WHITES NOW, but not quite the big thing Crazy Horse and Worm and Hump had thought would come. It was a kind of curling around the edges of the Lakota country, a probing and a feinting and a fending like two opponents unsure of themselves. The whites were tired after their big war, and many of their soldiers deserted when told they were to be sent against the Indians. Several attempts were made by the Indians to lure the soldiers into traps, at Julesburg and at the place called the Platte Bridge where the Holy Road and its wagon trains came across the river near a range of high hills, but too often the young and foolish warriors, anxious to get at the enemy, broke through the ranks of Akicitas and attacked too soon, giving the soldiers time to escape. Hump and Crazy Horse and other leaders were furious at them, but the warriors seemed to learn very slowly that strict discipline was necessary in this bitter war. Perhaps the biggest thing that happened was the rescuing of several dozen Indian families that were being marched east from Laramie by the soldiers toward the forts, to be herded and guarded like tame cattle. At Horse Creek the free Indians came in the dawn, gave guns to some of the captured ones, killed the little soldier chief and several of his soldiers, and got the captives away into the northern hills.

It was a time of great roving camps, the Lakotas, Cheyennes, and Arapahoes coming together like angry wasps after their nests have been disturbed, and sending out war parties on all sides to attack forts and wagon trains and isolated ranches.

It was at Platte Bridge that a sad thing happened, for here the Oglalas saw their young friend, Casper Collins, now a little soldier chief, riding toward them through an assemblage of Cheyenne warriors, shouting *"Hou, Kola!"* And they let him through their ranks to protect a friend, but he chased down the road to try to rescue one of his men and was caught up again by a cluster of Cheyennes, wild to revenge Black Kettle and the Sand Creek Massacre, so that he went hopelessly down under their lances.

"Another good one gone of the very few the Wasichus have sent us!" mourned Crazy Horse to

Hump, and the older warrior bowed his head and struck his heart, for he too had loved the brave young man.

Worm and his wife were worried about their two sons—Little Hawk, so reckless that it seemed that any girl who married him would soon be a widow, and young Crazy Horse, who had disappointed his parents by not courting through to marriage with the pretty younger sister of Yellow Woman, the Cheyenne he had saved after the massacre at the Blue Water.

Then came the time of the great ceremony to select the shirt wearers, the assistants to the chiefs. It was an old-time custom nearly forgotten, but taken up again to try to bring unity and strength to the people. First there were four shirt wearers selected to help the seven old man chiefs, called the Big Bellies. And when the beautiful shirts made of mountain sheep skins were held out in the great council tipi, many gasped to see that the shirt with the most tassels, each counting a brave or good deed, was given to young Crazy Horse, he who alone of all the others hid his head in shyness and acted as if he did not want this honor. Of the other three, Young Man Afraid, son of the great chief Man Afraid, accepted his shirt as something due him because of his great family, while Sword, son of Brave Bear, the Oykhpe chief, looked with thankfulness and respect at the seven who had given this honor, and American Horse, son of Sitting Bear of the True Oglalas, could hardly keep his face from bursting with pride as he sat up very tall and straight.

Worm and his wife, proud though they were, hoped that their son would listen to the old men who told the shirt wearers they must be worthy of this great honor and these sacred shirts by guarding the people from all harm and treating all with the greatest honor, even those who spoke or acted against them.

They heard the joyous trilling of the women, and the shouts of the warriors at this choice of four fine young men. And the people's spirit seemed to rise like a great wave, so that on that day all the Oglala acted as if they were one people. But some noted that Woman's Dress, son of Bad Face, moved away from the great lodge with a face dark as the thunder clouds, for he had hoped that the power of his father and of Red Cloud would get him a sacred shirt. Even later, when two other shirt wearers were named, Big Road and He Dog, Woman's Dress was again not mentioned. Crazy Horse was especially happy for He Dog, his boyhood friend, and he felt the two would have much to do with each other and in the fighting in the years ahead.

Other bad things besides war and buffalo killing came from the Wasichus. There was the spotted sickness and coughing diseases that hit especially the weak ones, the children, so that many
died in the cruel winter of 1865–66, when the
snows bound the land more than usual and no
warm chinook wind came to break the ice early
on the medicine waters.

And perhaps because he was sad over the
death of young ones of the Lakota and wished he
had a young one of his own, born in love to see a
better day and perhaps to help to herald it in,
perhaps because of all this he came again and
again to the camp of the Bad Faces, to be able to
talk to Black Buffalo Woman, even though the
women were now gossiping and No Water was a
disapproving shadow in the background. But her
clear eyes answered his and her voice was strong
with feeling. He could not understand why he
had lost this one whom he had teased into smiling and laughing with the tip of a feather so long
ago when she was a baby. Had she not, by look
and murmur, promised herself to him inside the
blanket long before No Water came between
them? Was it not Lakota custom that a married
woman had the right to leave one she did not
love?

In the winter of 1866–67 came the Battle of the

Hundred Slain, the fight the Wasichus called the Fetterman Massacre; a good winter to be warm in the tipis, for it was the coldest even the old ones had seen. In the beginning of the Moon of Popping Trees, Crazy Horse felt the strange thing come again that was part of his growing medicine, the warmth surrounding him even on a cold day, as if the heat were blowing out from his body and driving away the cold so that the snow flakes did not touch him. It was like the feel he had for bullets and arrows, ghostly streaks coming through the air that he could dodge with a twist of the body before they could strike him, knowing exactly where they were coming.

Late in that moon the combined tribes of the Oglalas, Minneconjous, some Brulés, Cheyennes, and a few Blue Clouds or Arapahoes made a decoy and a trap outside Fort Phil Kearny at the headwaters of the Powder River. As usual, Crazy Horse led the decoys, pretending to attack the fort and then running away when the soldiers boiled out in answer to the three shots for help that came from their wood-gathering detail. It looked like a hundred soldiers coming out of the fort to save the wood-gathers, and he knew that the little soldier chief who led them was Captain Fetterman, the one who had boasted he could take fifty men and ride through the whole Lakota nation. Let him come now and see what he could do! The decoys retreated and the soldiers followed them, coming faster and faster until Crazy Horse had to whip his horse down over the Lodge Trail Ridge and into the little canyon of the Peno where the warriors waited.

When both the riding and walking soldiers had rushed into the trap, Crazy Horse signaled his decoys to criss-cross their trails, and the warriors, seeing the sign from their hiding places, came rushing out of the brush and trees with a great shouting. Crazy Horse was in the thick of it from then on, hearing the whine of bullets and the swish of arrows, the white soldiers backing up and backing up, as their numbers fell, trying to find a place to make a stand, some brave men among them fighting valiantly on the edges to protect their brothers and going down under the clubs and arrows and bullets. A Minneconjou was the first to charge right through the main clump of whites, counting coup and clubbing as he went, and Crazy Horse followed, the wild cries around him like a great roar mixed with the screams of wounded horses and men.

Then all the soldiers were down except for a last group of cavalrymen who had let their horses go so they could climb quickly up behind some rocks on top of a little icy hill. Now the warriors crept over the ground toward them, their breath and even their hot bodies steaming in the cold. *"Hoppo! Ho! Up!"* shouted Hump and Crazy Horse when the time was right, and up the warriors rose in a wave that engulfed the last soldiers in a final flash of flame and smoke, the good back-loading rifles of these last ones shooting fast, but not enough to stop that charge. Then there were only the final deaths, the groans and deep sighing of wounded Indians, and the wind that told of a blizzard coming, whining in the leaves of the pines.

The new grass and the warm sun came late that spring of 1867, and there was not much fighting for a while. But in the beginning of the Moon of Cherries Black, the Lakotas and their allies had a taste of future difficulties with back-loading guns when the wood-gatherers from Fort Phil Kearny were surrounded in a wagon-box fort they had made on the hill and stood off repeated charges of the warriors with their repeating rifles.

"We need those guns," growled Hump to Crazy Horse, "or they will slaughter us like the buffalo!"

In the Moon of Calves Growing Black Hair, Black Buffalo Woman had her third baby, but the gossips talked when Crazy Horse came often visiting to the village of the Bad Faces, and brought the elk teeth he had got from a herd the previous winter to make into necklaces for her already abundantly laden woman's buckskins. In the camp of the Hunkpatilas, the mother of Crazy Horse told her husband, "No good will come of this love for a married woman. It is not our son of the great dream who does this, but one trapped by a girl's glances like a love-sick youth."

In the new year, at the end of the Moon of Snow Blindness, Crazy Horse, his brother Little Hawk, Little Big Man, and American Horse, led out a war party when they heard about a Lakota killed by a soldier down at one of the trading posts along the Holy Road. American Horse and his friends knew the owners of the Horseshoe Ranch along that road, and suggested they stop for a visit and to get a little powder. When they were met by bullets instead of friendship, the warriors circled the ranch house and fired the stables and the stockade, keeping the ones inside away from water. Twice the Lakota went away and twice they came back, finally firing the main house itself. On the second morning they found that all had burned down, but the whites had escaped through a secret tunnel to an outbuilding, got to a nearby ranch where there were horses, and taken off down the Holy Road toward Laramie.

With a whoop the Lakota war party was after them, Little Big Man noisiest of all and Little Hawk riding the most recklessly. Soon they had them partly cornered on a pine-tipped hill, and in the fight that followed, one by one was killed, including a man who bravely pulled an arrow out of his eye. Finally there were only four left, and these four stood stalwart, ready to die.

Suddenly Crazy Horse looked at the sky and saw the great Circle of All That Is, the earth forming its circle too, and the white-throated swifts making smaller circles high in the blue. And he realized that the whites too were men, children of the Great Spirit, and there were some among them good and brave. He remembered also Bear Boy and young Casper, who had died senselessly because someone had given him an untamed horse. So he rushed his horse forward just as Little Big Man was about to pull the trigger on his gun, and called out: "Enough! These are brave men. We will let them live."

Now Crazy Horse put down his knife and gun and walked toward the four with his hands up-lifted in the peace sign. They held their guns on him, but he sat down in front of them without a sign of fear, took out his pipe from its case, stuffed it with tobacco, lit it, and smoked to the seven directions, while the bloody, tired faces in front of him gradually relaxed, and they too took the pipe in the age-old sign.

"Enough brave men have died," he said, and made slow sign talk that said: "We can be brothers, one day, white and red. Let us smoke to that day."

So he let them go free, after they had agreed to give some of their supplies to the Lakotas. But he knew he would need to watch Little Big Man for a few days or there would be four scalps in that one's pouch!

Now the Wasichus, in the Moon of Tender Grass, were offering peace that many said was a good thing, saying all the land from the Missouri to the white peaks of the Bighorns would belong to the Lakotas and the Cheyennes, including the Black Hills and all the Powder River Country, as long as grass shall grow and water flow. Even Man Afraid went down to sign the papers, with Spotted Tail of the Brulés, as also did Little Wound and many other chiefs. But Crazy Horse and Worm said, "Why sign for something we have always owned?" And Red Cloud and Red Dog stayed on the buffalo ranges and did not sign, nor did Four Horns of the North, Sitting Bull, and Black Moon of the Hunkpapas. Only after the soldiers left the Powder River Trail, the forts empty and silent under the warming sun of the Moon of Shedding Ponies, did Red Cloud go to the fort of the Wasichus to sign that treaty that was to last forever, and give the red man a lasting haven of his own.

But it was not long before the people began to see that the peace was not as good as many thought. Soldiers kept the traders away from going to the Indians, and those traders that did get through were too often the whisky-peddlers who made the young Lakota men wild enough to do crazy things and even kill other Lakota. And the buffalo hunters were not only wiping out the herds to the south, but sneaking into the Lakota country every chance they had to get at the northern herds, using their many-shooting guns to hold off Lakota war parties that tried to stop them. So, even in the time of peace, the wasting away of wildlife and the power of the people was going on.

But the thing that drove Crazy Horse furiously into the hills to think alone in the Silence was the coming of two Bad Faces to the Hunkpatila camp to warn Worm that his son must have nothing more to do with Black Buffalo Woman or there would be blood on the trail. "A woman of our people has the right to choose another for a mate if the first has proven wrong," he told his father. But the older man shook his head.

"There is too much power where her feet walk," he replied. "There is Black Twin, brother of No Water, who is strong as a shirt wearer, and others who are powers among the Bad Faces, including Red Cloud himself, who are against this thing. Think well, my son, about the women and children who will suffer if there is more blood spilled among the Oglala!"

Crazy Horse listened reluctantly, and noticed the bowed head of his mother, whom he also knew felt Black Buffalo Woman was no longer the one for him. So for a while he tried to put aside from his mind those eyes that now always seemed to look toward him with longing. Yes, he thought, I must think of the little and the weak who would suffer if there is bad blood again.

But then came in the Moon of Shedding Ponies, of the year the whites called 1869, a great and successful expedition against the Crows, driving them back behind the Bighorn, laughing and mocking at them even at the gate of their agency where they ran to hide behind the soldiers. And from this trip many warriors came back, singing the praises of Crazy Horse and his powers, his wonderful way of leading in battle, daring the Crows to kill him until they feared him worse than a whole war party. But most of all they sang of the way he rescued the wounded and

carried them back to safety out of the cold breath
of death.

"Let all the peace chiefs go to Washington!"
the young warriors cried. "Here we have the true
Lakotas! *Hoye!*"

Crazy Horse felt his heart swell within him,
and he knew the time had come to stand firm
even before his father. Was it not time now that
one who no longer loved her husband should
come to the one whom she had promised herself
to in the long-ago? It had been a long wait!

He must have his own lodge now, separate
from his father, so he took a small lodge near the
camp of the Bad Faces.

Joy rushed within him when a few nights later
he heard the soft step of moccasins outside, heard
the flap lifted and knew the sweet sage and
woman scent of one he loved. She was against
him then, her heart fluttering, telling him in a
rush that she had left word for No Water that he
was no longer her husband (the simple divorce of
the Lakota) and had left her three children with
relatives. Now at last she could walk free with the
one she loved.

He was ready to take her with him in the dawn
on a small war-party with women along to go
west to the Yellowstone in search of the Crows.
Many warriors were eager to be with Crazy Horse
now and he had found several friends to go. So

she rode with him proudly that first day in the warm late Moon of Shedding Ponies.

He had forgotten his mother and father and even that Little Hawk was far to the south on a war party that he had asked Crazy Horse to go on. He had forgotten Hump who had asked: "Come north with me to join the Hunkpapa and the Minneconjou in a great strike against the Wasichu along the Missouri."

"No," he had said, "it is not time."

But Hump had growled deep in his throat, and Crazy Horse had heard him faintly say the forbidden words: "The woman always comes between men!" and he had known that his warrior father was speaking about Black Buffalo Woman of whom he had always disapproved.

But now on the Plains heading toward the Little Bighorn Crazy Horse had forgotten all this, for he was delighting to the nearness of one who now radiated not the shyness of youth, but the surer love of a knowing woman, and his heart was singing with the knowledge of her nearness like a cloud of light and joy. The question of trouble was way in the back of his mind now, as he swept his gaze back to meet the reward in her eyes, and the knowledge that she was his at last.

So it is often with a man before the darkness comes. On the second night the little party met a camp of friends, including Little Big Man and

Little Shield, brother of Crazy Horse's best friend, He Dog, who invited them to eat with them. They had started to dip their hands in the hot wasna stew and to put the food on bark plates, when a great shouting and other noise swept up to the tipi and the flap was torn back without further warning. Into the tent lurched No Water, swaying a little, his eyes red-hot as coals.

"Look at me! I have come!" he shouted, and pointed his revolver at Crazy Horse. The young Oglala jumped to his feet in a flash, drawing his knife, but Little Big Man grabbed his knife arm from behind and jerked it back just as No Water pulled the trigger. The crashing sound in the tent stunned everybody and Crazy Horse felt a ripping across his upper jaw, the flashing fire that comes just before unconsciousness, and he fell forward into the flames.

As Little Shield and Little Big Man hastily pulled him out of the heat, No Water turned blindly and ran from the tipi, laughing like one crazy. And those who had heard of the dream of Crazy Horse knew that just as in the dream, one of his own people had held his arm while another Oglala attacked him. And when the thought came that he was dead because he lay so still, the roar of the warriors rose like a great wind, the women trilling the call to victory, for suddenly there were those ready to kill for Crazy Horse, and once again, as at the time of Bull Bear, thirty years before, the Oglala were cracking apart into two hostile camps.

"The Bad Faces, the Bad Faces!" some cried. "They have always been jealous of our Strange Man! It is time to kill!" Only Little Big Man was silent, for the eyes that looked upon him were dark with anger, and he slipped away to safety as soon as he could.

But No Water and his friends were gone when the warriors went looking for them, gone on swift horses to the south, making few tracks to follow because they rode in stream beds and rocky places, so that the warriors gathered themselves like a coiled spring, ready to go against the Bad Face camp itself. By the next day Worm had arrived and his brother, Long Face, and Bad Heart Bull came, with face long and sad, for it was he, he admitted, who had loaned the pistol to No Water to go hunting with, something he would never have done if he had known the true purpose. But No Water had seemed gay and friendly, with no hint of the darkness in his heart.

Then these three looked at Crazy Horse, lying still under the ministrations of the Medicine Man, who had sewn up the wound and placed warm compresses of healing herbs on it, saying "He breathes and is alive; he will be well again!"

For hours they watched like men made of

stone, but gradually the color began to come into the pale face, the young Oglala moved a bit and his eyes opened. He saw his father and the other older men around him and he began slowly and painfully to signal with his hands, being unable to talk.

"Let there be no war among our people because of me," the signs said. "Protect Black Buffalo Woman. She did no wrong."

So the old men called the warriors and talked to them quietly, telling them what Crazy Horse had said, and that he would live. Many made the deep growling in the throat that meant anger against No Water and other Bad Faces that had encouraged this thing, but finally all agreed to follow the wishes of Crazy Horse. Yet many knew there would be bad blood among the Oglala for many a day.

Crazy Horse had been moved a few miles away to the lodge of another uncle of his, Spotted Crow, where his mother and father also came to help him heal by their presence and the food his mother made for him when he could eat. And here he heard that Black Buffalo Woman had first been taken to the lodge of Bad Heart Bull and then finally back to the lodge of No Water where the warning was given that she was not to be harmed. And there she took up her woman's work again and gathered her three children around her. And all knew she would not belong to Crazy Horse beyond that short time they had been allowed.

So Crazy Horse now swallowed this bitter medicine, for he was blaming himself for coming near to destroying the unity of his people in this time when they were being attacked from every direction. Matters became worse for him when he learned that Little Hawk, his reckless younger brother, had not come back from the south where he had gone in a war party against the whites. One came from the south who was badly frightened because he said the white miners, the freighters, and the Gray Men (bandits) had formed a secret society to kill Indians. He feared they had gotten Little Hawk.

When Crazy Horse was well enough to use a gun again, though weak, they took him with a party north of the Yellowstone to hunt buffalo, and it was in this place under the blue sky and with the murmur of great waters that he heard at last from the war party of Little Hawk. The survivors came sadly into the camp one day and told how Little Hawk had been in a fight with the bad Wasichus who had sworn to kill Indians, how they had all raced their horses to get away from the hail of bullets, but found that Little Hawk was no longer with them. They went back to look for him and found him lying on the wet ground at a place where he had charged the party of whites in his reckless way alone.

They looked at Crazy Horse and saw his face darken as no man had seen it darken before, and they thought he was angry at them, and shrank before him, but he called them back with a voice that shook: "I am responsible for this and no other! He asked me to go with him, but I refused because I thought only of the woman!" And he turned his head away so none could see his eyes, and all quietly left the tipi. But when his mother returned later to prepare the food for dinner, he cried to her from his heart's depths: "*Why?*"

She said quietly, "You must understand that the Great Being did not want you to have this woman for a wife, for she turned away from you at the one moment when it counted, when she had to stand up and say her love for you was greater than the power of her relatives."

She paused now, and her eyes looked beyond the dinner she was preparing and beyond the tipi and beyond the camp circle. "Perhaps in another time such a one as she will be strong enough to choose and to be wife to an Itanca with great visions. And perhaps in another time men such as No Water and families such as hers will look beyond personal loss to the place in destiny of those they are close to. Perhaps another in another day, with your spirit, will be given one as beloved as Black Buffalo Woman who will in that time bear the children that have your spirit and your vision and can lead our people.''

He nodded slowly, showing he understood the demands of the times in which he lived, and drew his hand through his hair, then said only quietly to himself: I must think of my people first.

And as if she read his mind she said quietly: ''In the wild places you will have the dreams that tell you what to do.''

But the new way for Crazy Horse was not to start until one more act born of a depth of feeling beyond common feeling would shake him. Learning that one he had seen riding nearby on a golden buckskin was No Water, he leaped bareback on a fast gelding and took off in the direction he had gone. When he got near him, No Water began to quirt the buckskin frantically, and they raced over the waves of the grass until No Water reached the Yellowstone and plunged into the swirling waters. His horse was strong and bore him to safety, but Crazy Horse stood on the bank with his gun in hand and did not fire it. He knew that No Water would never come back again to a camp of the Oglalas that was near that of the Hunkpatilas.

He knew also that there might be trouble from

this act of his, and it happened when there was a meeting of the Big Bellies, the old men chiefs, and all but one of them, Man Afraid, were against him now because of the power of Black Twin and Red Cloud.

They said Crazy Horse had broken the rules of the shirt wearers by chasing No Water after No Water had sent horses to make up for the shooting. Fourteen armed men were sent to the lodge of Crazy Horse to ask that the Sacred Shirt be given back, but Man Afraid came along to see that there was no fighting.

Weeping, the mother of Crazy Horse went at his bidding and got the shirt to give to the men to take back to the Big Bellies, where Man Afraid shamed them all by standing up and saying loudly: "I have seen some very bad work tonight! No other man shall wear this shirt, for none will be worthy of it."

8

The Great Vision

IT WAS 1871, a year of pause and peace in the Lakota Country, when Crazy Horse went up alone to Bear Butte, the sacred mountain of both the Lakota and the Cheyennes, for a vision search. He chose the first half of the Moon of Making Fat, when the whole warm earth was waving green under grass made thick by the rain from the Thunder Beings, when the young antelope were playing among the hills, and the buffalo herds were like black earth clouds. He wanted it to be so, at the height of all the good things of the earth and sky, the bobolinks and meadowlarks trilling from bush and grass clump, the prairie dogs whistling their alarm when his horse came prancing past their clusters of holes and mounds, the swallows hissing through the air by his head, the grasshoppers and butterflies flashing everywhere, and the warm, warm earth and leaf smell rising up like a heady perfume.

He was leaving a good warm lodge behind him too when he came, not the home of his mother and father any more, but his own lodge and his own woman, Black Shawl, one whom He Dog and Spotted Crow and others of his good friends had found for him in Big Foot's band. She was prettier than he had expected, but what was much better was the soft, quiet way she had taken control of his lodge, her voice like rippling waters, the least touch of her hands filled with kindness and love. Yet they were hands used to hard work, the fletching of skins, the cutting up of meat, the carrying of buffalo stomachs filled with water from the nearest springs or creeks, the endless sewing of buckskin clothes and rents in the wall of the tipi.

It was a new experience for the lonely man to see one seated opposite him at the cooking fire, day after day, while smelling the good food preparing, and seeing her look at him with that liquid, dark look so like and yet so stirringly different from the look of a mother. It was good also to feel that there would be no trouble over this one, for she came free of any jealous husband, and a sense of peace and all-goodness flowed through that lodge. And now, as he rode toward the mountain, he knew there was another life stirring within this new wife.

There was another sense of goodness coming with him also, for he had become indeed Itanca, leader in the Indian way, one who watched over the camp as a mother prairie hen watches over her children—one who had become the protector, as the bull buffalo stations himself between the herd and danger. He experienced a wonderful pleasure in coming into the camp in the dawn or early evening, bringing meat to a lodge where there was a widow or where the man was too wounded or sick to go hunting. And the herds of horses he ran down or captured from the enemy Crows or Pawnees melted away like the snow, because he always made sure that each family had an extra horse to pull travois with or one to carry an old woman or man when the trail was long and tiring between camps.

Yet there was a strange and terrible uneasiness that drove him to go alone to the top of Bear Butte for a Hanblecheyapi, a vision search. Behind all the good things that had recently happened to him, back of the peace and warmth of the lodge and camp circles, the Wasichus hovered beyond the great circle of the horizon like the ominous gray cloud of a coming blizzard in the Moon of Frosting in the Lodge. The cold of this feeling struck into his heart even on this warm summer day, and he tried to lift it off and gather hope from the beautiful things of earth and sky that surrounded him.

"Crying for a Vision," the Hanblecheyapi means in the Lakota language, and the heart of Crazy Horse was indeed crying to the Great Spirit.

He remembered the tales he had heard of what had happened to the Santee Lakota to the east, to the Mandans, the Sacs and Fox, and the Iowas and Pottawottami. They dwelt now on little reservations in shacks of wood, not the proud tipis or birchbark houses of old. There they were servants of the white men, looked down upon and given cast-off clothes, while the terrible bottles of whisky and wine dragged them lower like a dark hand clutching the heart out of them, dulling the senses. Was this now to come to the Teton Lakota, a proud people who would also be beaten down by the endless waves of whites until the spirit was gone?

He shivered as he thought these dark thoughts and remembered then his father's words: "My son, when you go to the mountain-top to pray, cast aside from your mind all thoughts save thoughts of the Great Spirit, of beauty and of strength. Call on Him for help for your people and for yourself so you can help your people. Purify the very breath you breathe with thoughts of the spirit until your thoughts rise like the eagles into the sky, up and up to be one with the Sun and the One Who is Behind the Sun. Be humble as the earth before all things, and when you have left the voices the body listens to, let the Spirit of Being flow into you until the secret Voice whispers to you through the needles of the pines the meaning of your life and what is to be.''

So he drove the darkness from his soul as the great bear drives the wolves from the carcass of the elk he was killed, and he galloped his horse to the last level spot on the side of the mountain where a little stream tinkled down over the rocks and a cluster of cottonwood trees hid a small vale filled with lush grass like a jewel, where the horse could be hobbled safely out of sight from a war party far below. Leaving his horse here, he took only his sacred pipe, a buffalo skin robe, some tobacco, a little food to be offered to the spirits, a bundle of the sacred sagebrush, four wild cherry sticks, and four banners of yellow, red, black, and white to tie to the sticks that represented the four sacred directions.

The climb up Bear Butte was like climbing a ladder up into the sky, there being places where the rocks formed steps amidst the pines. He knew he was going to a spot where few other men had ever dared to go for a Hanblecheyapi, a place so sacred and so dangerous it was whispered that lightning from the Thunder Beings had struck down those who dared to stay there, so that most vision seekers made their quests somewhere on the safer slopes below. When he reached the top, the glory of the earth was spread beneath, the waves of emerald green grass rolling to the east and north and south as far as eye could see, while to the southwest the great dark bear humps of the Paha Sapa filled the edge of the sky like dark thunderheads. It was as if he were alone at the center of the world, and his heart swelled as he turned to see the lovely green earth far below and the sacred circle of the sky coming down to meet the sacred circle of the earth. Here, if anywhere in the world, he thought, the Great Spirit can come to speak to a man who is a true seeker.

He made a circle about himself of the sacred pipe tobacco, made mainly of the leaves of the red willow and kinnikinnick, spread his sagebrush over the sharp rocks for a bed, and placed his yellow-, red-, white-, and black-bannered prayer sticks of wild cherry wood pointing to the four directions. The food and his loin cloth were placed outside the circle, but the buffalo robe lay beside the sagebrush for use when the cold winds of night would come. Next he took hold of the bowl of his pipe in his right hand and pointed the

Heralding the Sunrise, *by the artist Frederic Remington.*
"His heart swelled as he turned to see the lovely green earth far
below and the sacred circle of the sky. . . ."

stem to the west, crying the sacred song: "*Wakan Tanka onshimala ye oyate wani wachin cha!*" (O Great Spirit, be merciful to me that my people may live!)

Then he walked out to the sacred pole on the west and cried again the song, but here he added a variation of his own choosing, singing: "O Thou where the sun goes down, send me courage that I may be always brave for my people and protect them in danger." Then he returned to the center again.

Next he pointed the stem to the north, crying the usual song, but out at the north pole he sang also: "O Thou Giant of the North, give me of Thy great strength that I may help my people."

To the east, besides the holy song, he sang: "O Thou where the sun rises, give me of Thy purity and wisdom, that I may be like the new snow and the fresh spring water in my heart, and that I may be wise like the great chiefs of old who led the people in the holy ways."

To the south, besides the holy song, he sang: "O Thou producer of green plants and all good growing things, help me to grow in the spirit until I can lead my people where they will be safe from the Wasichus."

Now he pointed his pipe stem down to the earth, and sang: "O Thou Mother Earth, make me humble as you are when the feet of men walk upon you, yet give me your power to grow in the spirit.''

Next he pointed his pipe stem up to the sky, saying after the sacred song: ''O Thou Who art the Center of All Things that Are; come to me in vision that I may know what to do for my people.''

Last he swept the pipe stem around in a complete circle and pointed it once more to the sky, crying: ''O Thou Sacred One, Wakan Tanka, I send my spirit up to Thee. Send it back to me that Thy power may be within me, not for me, but for my people.''

Having thus sent his cry to the seven sacred directions, he was going to start all over at the beginning, as all the old ones did, but a sudden thought came to him, and he cried in a loud voice: ''O Thou Whose voice calls to me in the leaves of the pines, I have cried to you for the seven sacred circles, but tell me what is the meaning of the two circles yet to come?''

And he trembled for a minute in sudden fear, for he knew none of his people had asked this presumptuous question before. Then he gripped his pipe bowl hard once more, swung it to the west as he had done in the beginning, and started once more to make his motions toward the seven directions, and his songs. But at the end of the seven, as before, he asked his question about the eighth and ninth circles, and this time he was not afraid any more.

So the sun swung across the sky and down until it ebbed its great red disk below the horizon, and the cool shadows of the night wind began to whisper through the pines. Now Crazy Horse drew his warm buffalo robe around his body and dropped down upon the sage to rest, but holding his mind like a drop of dew poised on the tip of a leaf as he lay relaxed. Whenever he felt rested enough, he would rise up once more under the circle of brilliant stars, sending his call out to the constellations of the west, the north, the east, and the south, then down to Mother Earth and up to Father Sky and finally, drawing the Spirit in the seventh direction, into his inner being.

When the dawn came it was first only a faint haze of light on the edge of blackness, then a growing ribbon of light around the rim of the world, then a dull red disk that touched the eastern edge of the vastness of the plains, then a sudden blazing glory that sent its vibrant colors across the sky and around the sacred circle of the meeting of earth and sky. And he knew, though he could not hear it yet, that the Great Spirit was talking to him out of the heart of the sky, the land, and the light.

So he prayed and sang now with a rhythm that was the rhythm of earth and sky, of wave and wind and cloud, of summer and winter and night and day, until all tiredness and hunger and thirst left him as if they had never been. Thus it went on through the hours that were no longer counted, but were only a smooth running like the wind, until late on the third day the great black thunderheads loomed to the west of him, forming armies marching eastward, until the Thunder Beings were talking above him in the darkening sky where the lightning flashed and flickered.

A shower of large hailstones came out of the sky, and a bolt of lightning leaped from the mountaintop only thirty feet from him, so that the thunder nearly broke his eardrums in one mighty clash, and then the hailstones were falling in myriads, but strangely none hit him or near him, and he felt as if suspended in space in the hands of the Great Spirit, so that he lay down as one tired would lie down in a bed at home after a hard day, but surrounded by peace. The fragrance of the sage grew in his nostrils until the odor was poignant with memories, and he fell asleep remembering the youth that had been Curly and the time the first vision came to him as he lay in the sagebrush under the cottonwood tree of long ago.

Now a sparrow hawk was fluttering above

him, uttering its *killy-killy cry*. And the cry turned into words that pierced his mind like waves of light, because there was no sound with them any more, but he understood their meaning.

"Look down!" the voice said, *"and behold what is to be!"*

So he found himself standing on the top of Bear Butte in the sunlight, and his eyes were such that he could see very far away things in detail, as with the far-seeing glasses he once took from a fallen soldier. So he looked below and there was a town of the white people there, with many houses, and he saw them busy with their work like many ants, but he felt a coldness from them that he did not understand until he saw on the edge of this town some poor shacks where Indians lived. The Indians wore old cast-off white men's clothes and their eyes were sullen like the darkness of a cloud where the Thunder Beings talk. He saw two of them lying still in the middle of the street where water puddles were, and there was about them the stink of too much whisky. An Indian woman was washing clothes in a backyard, by rubbing them on a rough board with soap, but there was about her all the weariness of the world, as if she could hardly move another inch. And he felt so sorry for her that he wanted to go down from his place near the sky and do the work for her so she could rest. So he knew that the old spirit had gone from these people and a great sadness came over him that he could hardly bear. And he knew who had caused this thing to happen, and who had put the wall between peoples, holding one down while the others took whatever they wanted. So his anger flashed like the lightning and he wished he grasped a gun, or even a lance so he could plunge down to attack. To die to save his people from this would be good. But the voice out of the light spoke again. *"This had to be,"* it said. *"But it will pass away, for all the people of Earth must gather together like the geese that fly together in springtime. . . . Watch now, and be alert to see!"*

He seemed to be breathing deeply then, as if he were sucking in the wind of heaven and his heart grew calmer, so that when he looked again, he saw not only the broken hearts and minds below him among his people, but also the few strong ones who somehow kept the spirit through all the bad times. *For there were old men and women there whose faces mirrored the clouds and the earth, and whose eyes had the light of the dawn, and he could see that they were passing on this spark to some few of their grandchildren.*

Now as he looked below he saw that there were black ribbons across the prairies where before there had been only green grass, and going along these black ribbons were little many-colored bugs that moved with great speed. And when he looked closer, he saw that there were white people and even a few Lakota traveling inside these strange swift bugs, and he saw that there were few horses any more.

Then the darkness all over the earth seemed to be increasing, but there were loud noises and whistlings and screams within it, and he sensed that most of the males of the earth were fighting one another. And he saw the emptiness and pain and tears in the faces of families, including Lakota families, and knew that somewhere their loved ones were being killed.

There was a time after this fighting when people ran about like crazy and seemed to be accomplishing nothing except putting up more buildings. But he looked into the sky and saw that there was an increasing number of large things that looked like birds with wings, but were not birds, that were flying through the sky, and in the nighttime they had many little lights. Then again came a great darkness and again a feeling of the males of the earth fighting and dying, while the very air seemed to scream and the explosions were so great that they rocked the mountains and he saw a place of many houses disappear beneath a great smoke cloud as if it had never been.

Now there came a new time after the second

great war, and he saw a new hope beginning to appear among the faces of his people, and some were gathering together for the dances in a new way trying to keep the things that deaden the minds, the crazy water bottles and the drugs that destroy, away from these gatherings, so that here and there the surge of the spirit was so strong that some of the men were singing strong heart songs and the women were trilling as in the old days. They were wearing better clothes now and living in better houses, but he could see also that there were still too many little walls, and one great wall yet between them and most of the white people.

Suddenly all the people's faces disappeared, and he saw the whole world as if it were in darkness, but there was a dawn light coming from the east and before it the daybreak star approached through the sky. It was a star with nine points, and he knew these represented the nine sacred circles, including the two new ones yet to come. Then he saw the sacred herb beginning its climb out of the earth. It was eerie to see the fresh green rising from a place of death, for it grew where a dead tree had been and as the dawn began to turn the whole east to glorious light, the herb grew again into the Sacred Tree of his people, with the branches full of flowers and singing birds, and below the tree, spirit people and animals and birds were dancing and singing as if they had all the joy in the world but could not contain it.

Then, behind this world of glorious light, which he knew was the real world of the spirit, he saw the dark other world filled with people as if in a swamp or quicksand, but some beginning to reach their hands out toward the light, some seeing it and some not seeing it, as with men on the trail of a mountain lion, some seeing the little places where the paws bowed down a grass or herb and others not seeing these places at all, but only seeing the rocks and plants in a haze like one mass.

"Do you see it?" some people were saying to others. "Do you see that light coming? It is so wonderful!" But other people looked and shook their heads and their faces remained sad, or dull and ugly. They grimaced as a hermit does who has been shut in a cave of darkness for years and resents bright light which he is unable to deal with. Only slowly can his eyes and mind take in and understand any light.

The faces of the ones more ready were slowly turning to beauty and glory. *Then he saw that these people were already dancing in the spirit under the sacred tree, for the dawn of understanding was penetrating and they were ready. There were many dif-*

*ferent faces under that tree, so he understood that it
was a tree too big for just his people alone, but included
all races of all men, white and yellow, black and brown
or red. And their faces were full of laughter and joy.
And they formed one circle of one people, united
though different in a strange and sacred way that he did
not quite understand.*

When he awoke on the high top of Bear Butte,
it was early daylight and the sun had just tipped
the horizon to flood the earth with light. Down
the slope the rock wrens were singing as if their
hearts would burst, chanting their varied *"tu-tu-
tu, chrr-ee, chrr-ee, chee-poo, chee-poo, chee-poo!"*
with such joy that it seemed that what would be
was now here. Weak from fasting, he had been
allowed the gift of eternity. Time and space had
dissolved. Only as his consciousness returned to
the times of 1871 and the place on top of Bear
Butte did he realize the long and hard stages
ahead until the light would come.

9

It Is Hard to Hold to a Great Vision

WHEN CRAZY HORSE told his vision to his father, the older man smoked for a long time in silence. He thought of the other hill where they had sat together, long before. He thought of the doe whose son nearly outran her. The man he called son had been given a vision greater than any he would have. And the son's understanding might one day outreach that of the father. So it was more to himself that he at last spoke, and also because the son must discuss his vision.

"There is both good and bad about this vision. The bad is that you saw our people conquered and living in the square gray houses that Drinks Water saw. You saw the crazy water hurting many, and you saw the Wasichus running the lives of the Lakota as if they were the spotted cattle. But you saw also that some still carried the great dreams in their secret hearts, and sang them when they were alone, so that not all our people became like the black ants when the red ants make them slaves. Out of the darkness the light of a new day finally came shining, and then these bearers of the secret helped spread that new light to all peoples.

"This I see we must do. We Lakota are the most powerful of the Plains tribes. We must try to make allies of other tribes and raise all our strength to stop the white men, even though, in the long run, we cannot win. We must because the story of our courage and our fighting will be sung down the years ahead to give heart to all the Indian peoples, for they will know our warriors died bravely and we will show that the Wasichu can be defeated. And there must be some among our leaders whose honor and courage stand out like shining stars in a dark night, keeping the spirit alive among the few until the New Time comes. Gather around you, my son, while there is still time, all the young people you can. Tell them the stories of the great dreams and the great heroes, and be yourself, while humble, one to whom they can look for guidance, one who speaks always with the straight tongue, one who is never afraid, and one who fights always for justice for his people regardless of what may happen to himself or what others may say."

Again Worm smoked and was silent, while his son bowed his head in deep thought. Then the old holy man spoke for the last time: "The great hope is that one day there will come to us white men and other peoples too, seeking the wisdom of our people, seeing the circle of earth and sky, seeing the hoop of all men under the Great Spirit. For a while we will not dare talk to most white people about these things, for they will laugh at us as the silly young jackrabbit laughs at the wise coyote, because he thinks that since he can run faster he can always escape.

"But your dream tells us there will come a time when more and more will see the wrongness of the ways of the Wasichus, even among their own people. More and more will see they are out of touch with the Great One above, even though they bow before him and say their prayers, and have buildings where they worship Him. More and more will see they have lost the circle and must find it again, and that the Indian peoples can help them, for we are of the earth and sky and some of us will never forget this. And when we help them, all men that are still alive after the times of trouble that must come will come to- gether in One Circle and we will be one people, filled with the glory of the spirit. So did the vision of White Buffalo Calf Maiden promise us, and so also does your vision. Be brave then, my son, and take hope, even when the darkness comes, for does not the sun always rise again after even the darkest night, and does not the beautiful warmth of springtime come again with its flowers and singing birds even after the coldest winter?''

Crazy Horse had always been interested in the youth of his tribe, stopping to speak to them with words of encouragement at their work or games, and joining in telling them the great stories of the people. But now he became far more active than before at this, so that the younger Black Elk, or Fire Thunder, and many another boy, and sometimes girls too, would come to his lodge, to sit in the sacred circle with the firelight playing over the bronze faces and the dark eyes both intent and shy. Though his voice was quiet, it was also vibrant, and he used his hands when he spoke as the eagle uses his wings to signal to his mate, so that there was something about those evenings around the fire that was full of magic.

Back in the shadows Black Shawl was a presence, calm and adoring, her eyes watching her husband, intense as any youth, but her hands busy when the time came to pass hot tea or coffee, and the good cooked meat.

The time came also when she was absent for a little while from the camp circle, coming back with a new voice that cried to the earth and sky until the gentle crooning soothed it, for to Crazy Horse a girl child had been born. And this girl indeed became the very life of his heart, for she grew to be a sweet child with pale brown curling hair like her father in his youth, and the far-seeing eyes. In those eyes were the meaning of her name which her father gave her, saying she would walk in sacred ways. She grew big enough to love to ride on his back and kick his ribs as if he were her horse, and laugh with a delight that sent his heart to racing. But, as she grew a little older, he saw both the tiny girl and Black Shawl coughing with the white man's disease that eats the lungs, and a dark shadow was over him then with every passing day.

Yes, and it was a bad time for the people too, with storms of disagreement rising between those who wished to live near the white men and be given food, and those who still sought the free way of old, the life with dignity. The old chiefs' society was long gone now, for those men, faced by the hunger of their people and the closing-in horizon, had taken what they considered the lesser of two bad choices and had moved into the agencies to fight for the doles of food and clothing the agent gave them.

But worst of all was the shrinking of the buffalo herds, growing less and less numerous so fast that the headmen and the medicine men spent many nights talking over what could be done.

But Crazy Horse was gathering slowly a nucleus of fighting men around him, drawn in by the tales of his bravery in battle and by the way the bullets never hit him, by his ability in avoiding the Wasichus who sought him, by the way he saved the wounded ones, and by his wisdom. So one by one young men came away from the agencies to join him, to be with one who preferred the life of the plains, hard though it was to find food, preferring it to the tame way where the Wasichus ruled. He taught them to search for visions with the Hanblecheyapi, to find help from the powers of the universe, and he taught them a new tactic against the armies of the Wasichus.

So they practiced hour after hour, both on horse and on foot, until they moved as one man, and Crazy Horse taught them special signals by whistle and arm that they learned to obey instantly.

"So do we move as one," he told them, "and yet each alone in a way to strike the enemy with fear and to hold the trigger finger, for we have few bullets ourselves and they must be used wisely."

"Hoh!" shouted the young warriors, and they made the sign of unity, the hoop against the sky, feeling now that under Crazy Horse there would be more hope against the whites who had spent centuries building unlimited war machines while the Lakota had been building spiritual union with All That Is. And Crazy Horse looked at them and their eager eyes and was heartened, but deep within he knew many a brave one would die.

Then he came home one day with a war party that had been against the Crow, one of the battles of survival in the clash for the few remaining buffalo ranges. He knew when he saw the camp of his people that a bad death had come. His heart seemed to move to his throat when he drew near and saw the torn clothing, the blood drying on the arms of the ones who had offered the sacrifice of their flesh, their most personal gift, in sympathy, all women, their faces broken with mourning.

"Be strong, my son," said Worm when father and son met. And slowly the father and mother told him how the coughing disease that came from the Wasichus had weakened "They Are Afraid of Her" until at last the final spark of life left the little girl that was his daughter. He knew they did not want him to go, but he had to see her even in death and he rode away across the prairies, hunting for where they told him the burial scaffold rose toward the sky. And, for a while as he rode, a terrible rage followed the blood through his body, causing his hands to clench until the nails bit into the flesh, and he wished he could kill all the Wasichus who, uninvited, visited their darkness upon his people. When he saw the scaffold, the little bundle, the beloved buckskin doll tied tight against it, and the rattle and other toys, his father's heart broke as does a great flood when the Thunder Beings fill the sky with rain and the deep beat of their drums. He flung himself on the ground and wept until all life seemed as empty as a broken gourd or a prairie chicken egg the ants have sucked dry.

A day and a night and another day passed while he lay there, but at last the blood of life moved through his veins again and he knew the call of his people came to him over the far hills. "They Are Afraid of Her" would be out of reach of his arms, but there was still a great task to do. So he rose as does a wounded bear, but the wound within him was deeper than any wound of the flesh and would take longer to heal.

He came home to the bad news that Custer and a thousand soldiers and civilians, plus fifty Indian scouts, had been to the Black Hills and had found gold. Worse still was the news that the Lakota had been so short of ammunition they had not dared to attack the long army train, and Custer had come out scot-free from his invasion of Indian lands without permission. "Gold and Custer in the sacred Paha Sapa!" exclaimed Crazy Horse. "The chiefs are mad to let him get away with this! Now the Wasichus are sure to come like a great flood!"

Far off in the agencies the young warriors seemed to hear his cry that hot summer of 1874, and many came to join him. But it was too late. Already Custer and his troops had escaped back to safety. But in the Moon of Colored Leaves and the Moon of Falling Leaves he led war parties into the Black Hills, the Sacred Paha Sapa, and they came back with pack loads of food and ammunition and many white men's guns that had belonged to miners foolishly after gold, in land that by treaty belonged to the Indians "as long as rivers ran and grass did grow."

He heard with dark anger of the herds of cattle driven north and west to feed the Indians at the agencies, and how half or more of the animals were stolen or sold along the way so that the pitiful herds that finally arrived were hardly enough to keep a small band alive. And what of the little ones and the sick, he thought, hearing also of the many new crosses made on the bluffs where the burial parties dug every day that winter. Then worst of all the word came that the

General George Armstrong Custer, photographed in 1872. Eleven years earlier, at age 23, he became the youngest brigadier general in the Union Army. In 1867 he was court-martialed for disobeying orders and suspended for one year.

Wasichus were saying they wanted to buy the Black Hills, and the uglier hidden word that if they were not sold them, they would take them anyway with the army. So again the words of white men and the papers they wrote on were nothing but lies, and the Lakotas knew that many were laughing behind their hands at how the Indians had been tricked.

And the choice was diminishing. Beg for food from the Wasichus or hunt game that soon would not be there.

But for Crazy Horse and his warriors and the women never far from them, there was yet only one trail, the one of the plains. The year 1875 was the last year of peace, but it was a bad peace, because already the agency chiefs, Spotted Tail and Red Cloud and the rest, were being threatened with stopped supplies if they held out any longer in selling the Paha Sapa, and even all the lands between the Paha Sapa and the Bighorns, so that the good buffalo country of the Powder and Tongue Rivers and the Rosebud would be gone from the Lakota forever. Lots of money, many presents, enough food for everybody for seven generations, the commissioners said, as if this were real value for that sacred land! Be wise, they told the indignant Lakota leaders, meaning: ''You are going to lose it anyway, for the armies of the whites can take it from you if they want to, so why not get the money and food and goods now?''

''The Eagles have turned into vultures,'' said Touch-the-Clouds of Lakota leaders forced into this position. The Minneconjou son of old Lone Horn of the north added: ''My father died too soon to see this happen. He went alone into the prairie and died quickly in the strange sacred way, as some of the old ones are doing now to show that death is better than slavery to the whites.''

Crazy Horse could only look at his tall friend, whose head topped all the other Lakota, and nod his head. But he could not let his heart sink like a stone. He had to think of the people, and so he counseled with his friend and others about how they could stop this sickness of the spirit.

Then one day Little Big Man came running by in the Moon of the Ponies Shedding Hair, a gun in his hand and shouting: ''There is a black robe coming over the grass toward us alone. I am going to kill him. He comes to weaken us with words!''

Crazy Horse lifted his arm commandingly.

''Let him come!'' he said. ''If we are not strong enough against his words, we are not strong enough for anything.'' There was a time when the Lakota, close to a trustworthy Mother Earth, had welcomed these black-robed people bearing the sign of their Son born to a Holy Woman, and had accepted them, thinking of their wise Buffalo Calf Maiden. But when these people said the sacred things of the Lakota no longer had power and the Indians must accept the greater power of the white man's religion, the Lakota had looked at their holy hills and wondered. Could these white men be using religion to conquer the minds of the Indians and turn them into slaves, as had already happened in the east?

So Little Big Man had raised his gun, which now he lowered at the words of Crazy Horse, but his short, powerful body bristled with anger as he turned away, spitting on the ground.

But Crazy Horse watched curiously as the black figure came across the plain, his hand upheld with a wooden cross, its polish gleaming in the sunlight. When the white priest was invited into his tipi, Crazy Horse saw a man of middle years with a thin ascetic face and intense gray eyes that looked on the Lakota warrior without fear.

"*Hou, Kola!*" he said.

"Hou, Kola," replied Crazy Horse. "My lodge is your lodge. My wife will bring you food and drink and you shall find shelter here."

The Black Robe bowed his head and spoke in passable Lakota: "Your kindness to me will be remembered by the Great Spirit. I know your heart is good and that is why I have come to you. I come seeking peace for your people and mine, and also to offer you the help of the Master of Life, Jesus, who is the only born son of the Great Spirit, and who died for us that we might live again. It is Jesus who would have us all be brothers, helping each other in this land. I know also that there are great difficulties because there are bad white people who come to you with lies, who teach your people to use the crazy water that makes them mad, and who try to seduce your girls and women. I know for a truth that for every bad thing the Indians have done to the white people there are ten bad things the whites have done to the Indians. Yet I also know, as you know, that your little ones and your weak ones will be terribly harmed if there is war. And I know, as you must know by now, that the white armies are like the seeds of the grass, and they will come and come until you are no more if you try to fight against them."

"You speak words of wisdom," Crazy Horse replied courteously. "I know about your Master of Life, Jesus, for I have had the traders' sons read to me about him from your Sacred Book. I see from what they tell me that he, like our White Buffalo Calf Maiden, was also a Sacred Being, who has brought the Message of the Great Spirit. If he were here now he and the White Buffalo Calf Maiden would be one to us, and we would surely listen to him and believe in all his words.''

''Then,'' cried the priest with joy, ''you must already be a Christian!''

But Crazy Horse shook his head. ''Your sacred one foretold, even as did the White Buffalo Calf Maiden, that one day there would be peace between all peoples,'' Crazy Horse answered. ''But I am not a Christian in your meaning of the word. But your people have forgotten, or they would not be divided as they are so that you confuse the Indian peoples and divide them too, making us leave our Sacred Tree and Sacred Circle for your little squares of religion that rub and irritate each other.''

''It is true my people are divided by their religions,'' said the priest, bowing his head, ''and this is a very sad thing. But you must know that we Black Robes belong to the Catholic Faith, whose very name means unity for all Christians, and once all the Christians had this unity but men came along who divided them up so they are as they are today. Our purpose is to bring them all back together again.''

Crazy Horse was silent for a while, making markings on the earth floor of his lodge. Then he lifted his head and spoke slowly: "I know you mean well, my friend, and if other Wasichus could be like you and the few friends we have had among the whites, there would be no trouble between our peoples. But even the one your people tell us is the Great Father does not protect us from the lies and bad actions of those who work under him. You know that it was not many years ago that your people signed a treaty with us that we would own the land of our fathers from the White River to the Little Bighorn and that it and the sacred mountains, the Paha Sapa, would be ours as long as grass should grow and rivers run. But now we know that this was a lie, for they have found gold in our sacred hills and now they want all the land from Paha Sapa to the Bighorns.

"As for your Catholic faith, I am sure it is a good faith for you, and some of you Black Robes have been good to us and helped us. But there are many who call themselves Catholic who do not live up to these things you teach, and they hurt us as much as the other Wasichus by stealing our lands, hunting for gold where they have no right to go without our permission, selling our young people the crazy water, and telling us lies like the rest. So you can see that somehow what you teach is not as big as you say it is, for otherwise these walls between all the groups of Wasichus would not exist and they would be one people in one big religion as we were in the old days when we all followed the White Buffalo Calf Maiden and her teachings. You see, when unity goes from among the people in any religion, then so also goes respect for religion and for the great dreams among both your people and my people. So today your people, like my people, are following little things of the Spirit and not the big things that would bring us together."

The priest thought for a minute, then said boldly: "Yes, but Jesus and His teachings are the big things we are trying to get back to. When we all turn to Him, we will be truly united! Look to the Teacher, and not to the ones who forget His teachings!"

"My friend, you speak truth, but you have left out one thing. It is indeed true that Jesus was as big as the blue sky and as full of light as the sun, for I have heard his teachings, but he is not the only one who teaches this way, or the only Messenger from the Great Spirit. If he were to meet our White Buffalo Calf Maiden I am sure they would be too big for any walls such as are between your people and mine, for they would be one in the spirit. Both he and she said they would return again when the world needed them. But I do not think this means the same person coming back to earth, but that the same Great Spirit speaks through another of our two-leggeds. If they are to come back in a new human form it will be because the world needs something new for a bad time, something they did not teach, else their teachings would unite the earth. But this is a new age coming, and a new way must be taught to bring honor and glory to all people under a new spirit. I believe it is very possible this new spirit is in the world now and beginning to grow, because I have seen it in vision, but you and I will be dead before it comes here. We can only pray that it will come soon to help our children's children.''

''Cannot you work with me now to bring peace between our peoples?'' asked the priest.

''My friend, you still do not understand me, but it does not matter. There will be peace in a few years, but it will be the peace of the con- quered and the dead. Your people are like the great mountainside when it moves downward in the avalanche, and my people are the animals in the path of that avalanche. I could indeed make peace with your people as do the treaty chiefs at the agencies, and then there would be an end to this war, but it would be a peace of the conquered ones, and not a true peace at all. I, too, wish the little ones and the weak ones did not have to suffer, for I have seen their torn bodies and heard their cries. But there is a time when men must stand up and be counted as men, or the spirit dies. There is no peace with justice coming from your people to our people, for your leaders believe we are like the bugs they can trample beneath their feet. If we go down like bugs before them, then we will be remembered as bugs and our people will forget their greatness. We will be slaves in the spirit as well as in the flesh. But if we die with honor, fighting to the end against this great injustice your people bring to our people, then we will be remembered. Here and there some of our children's children, when they are men and women, will lift their heads and each say proudly: 'I am a Lakota; my people fought with courage and honor, and were conquered only because the Wasichus had superior numbers. So our spirit will come back again, and when the new light comes, our people will be in the forefront of the greatest of battles, the battle to unite the great circle of earth and sky and bring justice to all men.' ''

When Crazy Horse was silent, the priest found a new wisdom, for he was silent too, and when he left to go back to the Wasichus he left knowing there was no more to be said.

10

The Last War Cry

IN THE MOON OF FROSTING in the Lodge of 1876, word came from the agencies that the soldier chiefs of the Wasichu were demanding that all the holding-out camps come in from the plains and the hills in thirty days or they would be considered enemies. Crazy Horse and many more of those still holding out laughed at this. Even the young and strong with good horses could not make it with their lodges and weak ones in that time of unpredictable weather. Either the Wasichus were mad or they meant to force a war, and it looked like the latter.

But some got frightened for their women and children by the stories of the thousands of soldiers coming into the Lakota country from the east like the swarms of locusts in summer. One of these was He Dog, and it made Crazy Horse's heart sick to see this strong friend of his planning to take his group of lodges in to the whites. But Crazy Horse stood up in the council and said to let those who worried about their women and young ones go, for only those should stay who had strong hearts. So He Dog left one early morning during a Chinook wind that had dried snow off the ground of the Moon of the Dark Red Calves, and Crazy Horse felt there was a great hole in his heart, joined to the one left by another strong friend, Young Man Afraid, when he too had decided it was useless to fight the whites any more and had taken some of the Oglalas to the agency at Red Cloud.

Word came later that He Dog's group had joined Two Moons and his Cheyennes at the mouth of the Little Powder when a new snow came, and they were waiting there until the weather changed good again before going into the agency. Then in the middle of the Moon of Snow Blindness a scout came running into Crazy Horse's camp with news of people coming, poor and wounded and some walking with rag-wrapped feet through the snow. Crazy Horse set up a call for the women to start cooking food and gather spare blankets and clothes, then led the warriors out to find the Cheyennes of Two Moons and the Lakotas of He Dog coming in a long, partly broken line out of the south, a few warriors riding guard on the flanks and rear. It was a sad story they told of being struck in the dawn by a company of soldiers led by Reynolds, a little soldier chief under Three Stars, as they called General Crook. Somehow the warriors had managed to get the women and children off into flight with the horses, and had fought hard enough to keep the soldiers at bay until the full escape was made, had even captured some of the soldiers' beef herd in a backlash through the snow, but the lodges had been burned and much food and sacred things destroyed. Now He Dog and Two Moons and their warriors talked no more of going back to the agencies. They were in the fight that was coming in the summer, and in it for good.

As the weather changed and the sun came stronger up from the south, Crazy Horse could feel the spirit of his people growing, and he forgot for a while the dark days foretold in his great vision on Bear Butte. In the Moon of Tender Grass the horses too began to gather strength, as the holding-out Oglalas came together on the plains of the Powder and more of the Cheyennes and others of the Lakotas began to join them. Then the day came when the Oglalas met in council and chose Crazy Horse as their leader, so that a great shouting ran all through the camp, while the drums beat and the women trilled the victory

song. *"Hopo!* Let the whites come now!" the warriors cried. "We will make no more mistakes; we
have a leader who wins every battle."

Now in the Moon of the Ponies Shedding Hair,
with the blue-bright circle of the sky glorious
above the waves of emerald grass, the Oglala-
Cheyenne camp moved north and west to the
valley of the Rosebud, drawn by news that there
were good buffalo herds there. First they came to
the camps of the Hunkpapas, under Sitting Bull,
Gall, and Crow King, and then on together to that
of the Minneconjous, under Lame Deer and
Touch-the-Clouds, plus bands of Two Kettles, No
Bows, and Blackfeet, even Yanktonais, Santees,
and, out of the south, some Blue Clouds or Arapahoes. All these were gathering in the greatest
Indian circle most had ever seen.

By the beginning of the Moon of Making Fat
the great camp had rolled along to the headwaters
of the Rosebud. And there it soon stretched along
the river, further than the eye could see, with the
spirit blowing through it like a sacred breeze.
Here the people watching the Sun Dance saw
Sitting Bull of the Hunkpapas tear a hundred
pieces of flesh from his bleeding arms, fall into a
great trance, and come out of it to say he had seen
a vision of "many soldiers falling into the camp."

Now the young women were hunting turnips and other wild plants for food on the surrounding swales, and the hunters were bringing in antelope and buffalo haunches behind their saddle bows, until the whole camp hummed with prosperity and joy like a great happy bees' nest in the first good warmth of summer. It was a strength too great to be worried by the reports the runners brought in of armies of whites gathering to the north and east. The vast circle had good scouts this time, and there would be plenty of warning.

And there was something about the way the warriors tightened their bows and shined their guns that told Crazy Horse and the other leaders that the Lakotas and their allies were united and ready for war as never before. He was glad to have other chiefs listen eagerly to him when he told of the new methods of fighting the Oglala had developed, rather than curl their mouths down as some of the treaty chiefs did when they felt their power threatened. It was good to see the young men practicing the new way of charging and fighting, some of them pretending they were Wasichus when the war games were played until the shouting and swish and thunder of hooves through the grass sounded almost like a real battle.

Soon again the camp moved over the break of hills to the Greasy Grass or Little Bighorn, and spread along it for three miles or more.

It was an evening warm with the rustle of happy talk around many little fires, and heady with the smell of buffalo and antelope meat cooking, when some Cheyenne scouts came in from the Rosebud with tales of a great army under Three Stars marching there. So the chiefs gathered in council, the young warriors eager for an immediate attack, but some of the older men counseling waiting until the army came near and then forming a wall of Indians against them. Crazy Horse waited until the last of all and when he spoke, his quiet tone and his spirit soothed both the frightened ones and the too-hastily brave, so that they were brought together as one people.

"The camp will need to be guarded and this could be done by the older warriors and chiefs, while the rest of the warriors come across the hills to the Rosebud quietly so as to hit the army of Three Stars when it is all strung out on the trail. When we strike, avoid the strong groups that are gathered to make a stand with fast-shooting guns, and strike the scattered groups that are running or traveling, so that we suck off the others to bring help and so string them out to be attacked by other warriors. When you attack, drive through them as if nothing can stop you. If you do this enough, they will begin to get frightened and some will run. Then is when we can kill most effectively and save our ammunition by using war-clubs and axes.''

That night, the Lakota and their allies moved along north of the valley of the Rosebud, resting in the early hours to gather strength. It was dawn of a new day when the scouts went over the ridge toward the big bend of the Rosebud. And here they saw some Crow scouts of General Crook's command coming up the ridge toward them. As the Crows fled backward under the first bullets, howling their warning cries to the long ranks of soldiers far below, the Lakotas and their allies came boiling up to the ridge top until it was black with warriors staring down at the Rosebud and the soldiers. Here Crazy Horse cautioned them all to wait, resting their horses and luring the soldiers up to attack them, so it would be the horses of their enemies that would tire first. And so powerful was the command behind his quiet voice that the eager young warriors obeyed in a way they had not done in other battles.

So it began, the Battle of the Rosebud, when Indian chiefs outthought and outfought a white general, even though the general had more men and they were armed with ten guns to every one the Indians had. In that rough terrain of the high hills it became a big battle of many little battles, mostly hidden from each other, as the Crows and the Rees and other Indian allies of the whites came boiling up one slope while the white soldiers rushed up others, and then the Lakotas and their allies on the ridge tops closed down upon them like a whirlwind, coming quickly and circling with a concentrated force.

Somehow Crazy Horse, first on his pinto, and then later on his bay horse, seemed to be everywhere, his red calf-skin cloak with its white dots flying back from his shoulders, his single feather rising above the small stuffed sparrow hawk that rested on the back of his head, his sacred stone behind his right ear, and his body streaked with the sacred lightning flashes. Later white men who were to write about this and his other battles would laugh at the superstition of the Indian, who dressed himself in such a crazy way. But they would not understand the mighty power in these symbols of the greatness of the spirit that lay behind this man, his courage and fearlessness, his uncanny ability to dodge the bullets that came flying at him from every quarter, his quick mind that seemed to gauge and counter each move of the enemy. To the other Lakotas that day, and to their allies the Cheyennes and the Arapahoes, to see and hear Crazy Horse come up behind them with his cry of *"Hoka Hey! It is a good time to die!"* filled the blood with fire. To their children and their children's children, the man leading them today could never be killed by bullets or passing years.

His quick commands that struck instantly at the job each man had to do filled them with a great flash of the spirit and a courage so strong that it led many to deeds of supreme bravery and sacrifice. And always they knew that this Itanca was at every moment where the battle raged thickest, thinking of his wounded men and getting them off the field to safety, by himself or with the help of others. He had also an uncanny ability to seize a carbine or rifle dropped by a dead or wounded soldier, sweep it up off the ground at full gallop, ram out a jammed bullet, put in a fresh one, and pass it on to a surprised warrior whose own gun was past firing. And there were other leaders and warriors that day who did heroic deeds.

General Crook had made one bad mistake early in this battle. He'd fancied that the great Indian camp was only five or six miles around the next few turns of the Rosebud, and had rushed off eight troops of cavalry to attack it. The Indians let these troops pass up the valley, and then closed in to attack those who remained. It was a glorious fight, but by mid-afternoon the weight of fire-power on the white side was beginning to push back the tiring Indians. As they fell back, however, a miracle happened. It was Crazy Horse again coming to the thickest part of the battle, rearing his horse high while the bullets whistled around him, and pointing his finger forward. "Be strong, my friends!" he shouted. "Remember the weak and helpless ones at camp! *Hoka hey!* This is a good day to die!" And he charged almost alone directly at the enemy, his rifle cracking its death song even as he rode. Good Weasel and Black Bear, Fire Thunder, Bad-heart Bull and Kicking Bear, and others like them took up the cry: "*Hoka Hey! This is a good day to die!*" And suddenly there were no more sullenly retreating warriors, but a great wave that rushed forward upon the Wasichu, gathering power as they saw the soldiers begin to hesitate and turn. Then the Indian allies of the whites, the Rees and Crows, were running away too, and the Lakota war cries filled the valley.

Almost up to Three Stars himself, with his little group of soldier chiefs and traders' sons, the charge of the warriors came. But here the soldiers' lines were suddenly thickening, with reinforcements coming, including the returning troops that had gone up the valley, so Crazy Horse, with a wave of his arm and a shrill sound of his whistle, veered his warriors away in a sudden maneuver that caused the first volley from the bunched soldiers to go wild and the second to come too late.

Now Crazy Horse tried to decoy some of the soldiers into a trap up a turn of the valley, but the howling Crows warned the whites at the last moment, and the maneuver was lost.

Now the bullets were gone, the soldiers in too much confusion behind them to attack, the shoulders of the warriors drooping with weariness, and the sun coming close to the western hills. So Crazy Horse gave the signal and they left for the great camp, knowing they had given Crook a scare he would never forget, and that so many wounded and dead soldiers were left on the field that the thrust of the white army was blunted and thrown back even as the king bull of the buffalo herd throws back and drives away the brash young challenger, wounded and exhausted. And so it was, for the scouts the next day reported that Crook was retreating, carefully hauling his wounded out of the Rosebud country, not to be seen again for several months.

Back at the great camp on the Little Bighorn,

the warriors came to sing the hero stories of the battle, stories of Crazy Horse, but also of Gall and Crow King of the Hunkpapas, Touch-the-Clouds of the Minneconjou, and many wonderful Lakota, Cheyenne, and Arapaho warriors, especially perhaps the Cheyenne girl who had galloped her horse into the middle of the fight where her brother, Chief Comes in Sight, was surrounded by soldiers. She had helped him climb onto the horse's back with one sweep of her arm, and had taken him away with scarcely a scratch out of the midst of death, the great praising cries of the warriors ringing in her ears.

But Crazy Horse took no part in the celebration or story telling. He was up on a hill smoking his pipe in the far silence, thinking with pride of his warriors in the battle, but knowing that this was the last of the great years of his people and probably only one more battle was left to be won before the long darkness fell. And he was thinking already of returning to the Rosebud fight with some of the boys to gather lead and powder, abandoned bullets and guns, for the next battle. And there was a need for runners to go quickly with soldiers' pay money to the traders to get more guns and call the young warriors at the agencies, whose spirits would be lifted at news of

the fighting and who could get to the Little Bighorn.

Six days later, the great camp moved across the
Little Bighorn River to the west bank, the movement little more than a wave in the days of excite-
ment and joy at being all together and having for
a while the sense of the power of earth and sky.
So the fires flamed in the twilights while the great
stories were told and retold, and the young men
and women courted on the edges of the shadows,
watched alertly but lovingly by the old women,
and the boys and girls played by the river as boys
and girls always play but with the sense about
them of playing in the midst of the greatest time
in their lives, for even the small children had
heard that Sitting Bull's prophecy would soon
come true of the ''soldiers falling into camp.''

Never had a summer day seemed so beautiful
as that day around noon when the scout came
racing down from the eastern hills, shouting
across the river to the Oglalas: ''Soldiers coming!
Soldiers coming!'' Through the water he frothed
his horse and up the far bank, his own shout
suddenly drowned in the great roar of the people
awakening to danger, coming up out of the calm-
ness of the blue and golden day, the lazy sleeps of
some under packed lodges ended quickly by the

noise, the children no longer splashing in the waters, but screaming up the banks, the women who were digging for wild turnips in the fields to the west coming into camp with anxious crying.

Crazy Horse heard the sound, first like a drone, and then like the talk of the Thunder Beings, and his heart and blood and muscles gathered within him. "They dare to come into our land and our camp and attack us without cause," he told Black Shawl as she hurried to gather his equipment. "Now they shall learn what it means when our people are of one mind. Now the eagles shall gather!" And he had grabbed his weapons and was on his yellow pinto and away like a great wind, his "Hoka Hey!" calling the warriors. All about him they were coming, streaks of light in the rising dust, and he could see across the river the great dust clouds where the soldiers were riding. Then he saw that many soldiers had crossed the river and were attacking the camp of the Hunkpapas. Sitting Bull, Black Moon, and Gall were leading several hundred warriors in a stand against them.

From that time on the battle was so much like the first of his great dreams that he almost thought he was dreaming it again. Again there were the screams of horses and men in agony, and the feel that bullets about him were like streaks of light that his body avoided as the squirming eel avoids the spear of the fisherman. Again there was the howling of men in combat and the sharp cracking of rifles, the swish of arrows released from bows. He led his Oglalas to help the Hunkpapas in the first battle against Reno's men at the upper camps, drove them reeling back across the river where the clubs and knives of the Indians wreaked fearful havoc in the bloody waters, until the last body of soldiers escaped to the hills above while Crazy Horse shouted, "Save your bullets, my friends, whenever you can!" Then the cry came from the north of other soldiers about to attack the lower camps.

Now he was riding back hard with his warriors to the north, in time to see a very brave thing, four Cheyennes crossing the river, marching in a row up toward the ranks on ranks of cavalrymen coming down off the ridge in a cloud of dust and firing as they came. But the soldiers stopped, as if amazed at this brave thing, four against three hundred, and Crazy Horse had time to change horses. Black Shawl waited for him as a brave wife should. Then there were five courageous Lakotas joining the four Cheyennes and the soldiers' rifles suddenly puffed their smoke of firing again.

But Crazy Horse had seen that Gall and Crow King of the Hunkpapas, along with more Chey-

June 25, 1876: The Battle of Little Bighorn (or Custer's Last Stand). "And here or there you saw a Lakota or Cheyenne or Arapaho locked together with a white . . . , but it was also like a dream that passed swiftly and was no more."

ennes under Two Moons, were crossing the river now to the attack with a cloud of warriors, so he set up the cry *"Hoka Hey!* It is a good time to die!" to gather the Oglalas around him, and swept off to the north as a leading goose spearpoints a flight of hundreds in the springtime, so that they could catch the soldiers from the rear. Across the river, up the slopes, and around and over the high hill they swept, until they heard the crack of guns once more and saw clumps of soldiers before them, some firing from behind their dead horses and one large group where the soldier chiefs and some of their followers were making a last stand in the dust and blood of war.

Then the Oglalas sprang upon them, as the mountain lion springs upon the haunches of the deer, and they were through them and over them and charging back again as the whirlwind strikes from many sides at the same time. For a little while there were some of the Wasichus who stood up or crouched, still fighting bravely. And here and there you saw a Lakota or Cheyenne or Arapaho locked together with a white, the two like clawing bears, but it was also like a dream that passed swiftly and was no more. Suddenly Crazy Horse found himself stock still on his panting horse, and all about him a moaning and sometimes a shrill scream of a dying horse, but no more of the crack of guns, the swish of arrows, or the grunts of men fighting. Stunned for a moment at the completeness of their victory, the Indians looked at each other in disbelief. Then the shouts began to rise:

"We have won—the Wasichus are wiped out!"

Slowly Crazy Horse rode down the hill, to make arrangements about the wounded and to see what to do about the remnant of Reno's command, now combined with the company of Benteen and dug in along the ridgetop to the south above the river.

But the next day the great camp was breaking up and moving out, some into the Bighorn Mountains for a hunt and some to the south, for word had come of a new and bigger white army coming up the Little Bighorn, and the chiefs had no more heart for fighting. It was as if they knew the last days of glory had passed and now came the darkness. And this darkness soon rose over the land, after one last blaze of light when the warriors fired all the grass along the Greasy Grass so the horses of the soldiers would have nothing to feed on when they came, the pall of smoke rising to cut out the light of the sun above the Indians fleeing southward.

11

"The Old Songs Shall Die for Awhile"

"WHEN THE OLD SONGS DIE, the great dreams are forgotten; and when the dreams are forgotten there is no more greatness!"

Crazy Horse and Sitting Bull had one last talk before the two split up. Sitting Bull headed north with his Hunkpapas and some others, following a devious route to reach Grandmother's Land, Canada. But Crazy Horse would stay in the land of his fathers, as a wounded bear comes back to his mother's cave, for he knew that the Lakotas were wounded deeply, even though they had won the Battle of the Little Bighorn. He put it in words to Sitting Bull: "Our people are full of talk of the great battle, but all their thoughts are in the past, because they know, as we know, that with the death of our brothers, the buffalo, the Lakota too will be a dying people."

"The dark days are coming," agreed Sitting Bull, lowering his wise head toward the earth, "But I am hoping that in Grandmother's Land we will at least find white men with the straight tongue, and there they do not kill Indians without reason."

"I hope this is true, my friend, but I see only a long blackness coming for all of us before our great-great-grandchildren or their children shall see the light again. For myself, I must stay here in the country of my fathers and try to keep a spark of that light alive in some secret hearts."

The sacred pipe of Sitting Bull, used only at discussions of importance, turned in his strong but sensitive hands. He too had been told in vision that the new greatness would not begin to come until the time of the great-great-grand-children, he said.

As the older chief spoke, through the mind of Crazy Horse flashed quickly his vision of the time when the Great Spirit would make the whole earth one circle, and men of honor would take the place of those of dishonor. It was to be a time when the earth would be made beautiful again, and the two-leggeds, the four-leggeds, the winged, and all living things would find new life in beauty. Increasingly in the remaining darkening year of his life, Crazy Horse would wish his loved ones were living in those times.

Now, the visionary Sitting Bull, who had earned his name—One Who Stations Himself Between the Enemy and Those He Protects—and his younger chief friend wondered if the Wasichus could change, as the dark shadows fade under the light of the sun in a new morning. Crazy Horse told the older man, ''I see a time, after the sky has grown dark and ugly and the waters bad-smelling, when the young white ones will come to those of our people who still carry the spark of knowledge of unity with all that lives and ask for wisdom. In that day there will be some who carry the light and who will give it to them.''

For a little longer the two counseled quietly together. Then they smoked the pipe of parting, sending the plumes of smoke to the seven directions, to the east and north and west and south, to Mother Earth and twice up to Father Sky, the last time signifying the sacred connection of man to the Great Spirit.

Soon followed a bad time for Crazy Horse and his followers, a bad time that steadily grew worse, like that of a great wolf, the pack leader, when the hunters are closing in on him from all sides and there are many packs of dogs baying on his trail. One by one his followers go down, until he stands almost alone. And so it was with Crazy Horse, as his first vision had foretold.

It was true there was a killing of his followers by the guns of the white soldiers, or Indian scouts in their pay, as were the Oglala Sitting Bull and four other peace-seeking leaders killed at Fort Keogh by the Crow scouts in the Moon of Popping Leaves. News of the killing of Sitting Bull he was spared—came twelve years after his own violent death. But he saw the cold snowy time on the Tongue River, in the Moon of Frosting in the Lodge (1877), when the soldiers of General Miles, in their warm buffalo coats and many-shooting guns, drove the shivering Oglala out of the warm bluffs by the water and over the icy hills. But it was not this physical killing that really hurt him deep within; it was far worse to see the spirit of his people dying as they felt the white men closing in on them, and the buffalo and elk so hard to find that often the skin bags of the people were empty of food. He knew the people loved him for the way he somehow found game where no other hunter could find it, bringing in the blood-dripping haunches and tongues to the hungry at the time of greatest need, and the way he comforted the sick and the wounded, while his strange power made them feel protected in a way no other leader could. But he saw the deep shadows in their eyes when they watched him, and no matter how far he twisted and turned over the plains and hills to dodge the white armies, no matter how he tried to teach the people that this earth was theirs and the Wasichu had no right to it, he knew those eyes, even the most loyal, were saying, ''How long must we go on this way when there is no hope?''

So in the beginning of the Moon When the Ponies Shed Their Hair, with the green grass thick again in the hollows and the antelope flashing their white rumps over the distant plains, Crazy Horse led his band to a meeting with Red Cloud and others of those friendly to the whites. Here Red Cloud and his people brought with them many presents and many promises from Three Stars, General Crook, that the holding-out camps would be furnished with an agency of their own and all the food and clothing they needed if they would give up the war and come in. So Crazy Horse agreed, for the sake of his people, having a little flash of hope that maybe with peace, things would be better for them, and that he could fight with his wits instead of guns for justice.

But he soon saw, at the agency at Crow Butte under Red Cloud and the little soldier chief named White Hat, how vain that hope was. He came in with his seventeen hundred men, women, and children, the warriors riding proudly behind him and singing the great Lakota Song of

Peace so loudly that even some of the Loafers about the Fort took it up too and sent the echoes from the hills. Even then there was quick evidence as to who were his friends. The soldiers took away the horses from the new arrivals and passed them out among the friendly Indians. How eager then came these other Indians, who had given up the fight long ago, to claim their spoils of war!

"Like the wolves coming to take the meat from the dying bear," said Little Hawk, the uncle who had taken the name of the long-lost brother.

And from that moment on, the snakes of gloom coiled themselves closer and closer about Crazy Horse and his people. The whole atmosphere at Crow Butte was dark with unseen but deeply felt jealousies, bitter words told behind men's backs, and the constant scheming for power and money. He saw it in the whispers behind a held-up hand. He felt it in the hostile glances from other leaders. Worst of all was the helplessness and being forced to stay in one place doing nothing, as if they were locked in the cages they were told the white men kept wild animals in the city. He would go to council with White Hat about this useless waiting and their need for an agency, but the words of the Wasichu would run over the hills of the wars that were past and leave the valleys of the present unheard from, making Crazy Horse feel he was talking with a shadow when it came to the important things needed now.

Even when General Crook came, and there was a surge of hope that this Three Stars would do something with his power, the surge died like a little whirlwind on the plain. When Little Hawk, who represented Crazy Horse, spoke straight to the general's face and reminded him of promises he had made to find an agency in the north country for Crazy Horse and his people, Crook turned a dark glance on the stern old Indian and promised instead a last hunting trip to the north to get buffalo. Crazy Horse would have thought Three Stars as bad as the gray men who robbed the Indians, if he had not found out later that Three Stars did try hard to get that agency for the former holding-out people, but was stopped by higher orders; probably from General Sheridan, who openly hated all Indians. Yet what good were promises that could be taken away so easily? The powers among the Wasichu evidently thought the Indians could be treated like meadow mice trampled under the hooves of the buffalo.

But worst still was the great lie of Grabber, the half-breed interpreter, a man who had fled to both Sitting Bull of the Hunkpapas and to Crazy Horse, seeking protection when he had to run from the Wasichus because of killings. Now this man, who had been taken as a friend into the lodges and fed from the stewpots and the grill sticks, was working to build hatred toward Crazy Horse and his people among Wasichus and Lakotas alike. Was it because the treaty chiefs and the Loafers about the Forts had become frightened over the rumors that Crazy Horse might be made chief of all the Lakotas, and were using Grabber to build this poison against him? Crazy Horse lay on his buffalo robe in his lodge and stared up at the little patch of blue sky through the open tent flap and wondered how else it could be explained that Grabber had told the little soldier chief, White Hat, that Crazy Horse had said he would ''go north and fight until every white man was killed.'' How weary he was of this web of lies that surrounded him, the stink that lay over this permanent camp like an ugly cloud, this enforced idleness of his people when they had been used to a changing view of the wide sweep of the plains and the water rushing by from the hills, the song of the meadowlark and the clean beauty of the rainbow.

As he looked at the bit of blue above him, his spirit tried to go up and up out of the tipi and into the wide space of the sky. ''*Wakan Tanka*, Grandfather,'' he called softly, ''have pity on us, a broken people! Free us from this trap of the Wasichus; make us live again.'' And far up in the deep blue he saw a white-throated swift dip and swirl like a leaf caught in a whirlwind, then fly straight up like a bullet going into the farthest depths of heaven. And this sight of a creature of the Great Spirit who still had the freedom he had lost somehow gave him comfort and strength, so that a voice seemed to murmur within him like an echo of all his great visions, saying: "There is still the circle of heaven and earth. Yet a little waiting for your people, then what the Wasichus bring will be only a bad dream that shall pass away like a shadow that has never been. In that day some of the Wasichus too will learn the meaning of the Sacred Circle, and they will help your people change the earth to beauty."

For a moment he felt a flow of glory, a warm feeling all around him, and then he heard the stifled sound of Black Shawl, trying to hide her coughing under her blanket, and he knew again the deep sadness of the time in which he lived.

I shall die, he thought, in a time of darkness, but I shall at least die like a man and know that someday the light will come to my people again.

Perhaps he saw what was just around the corner.

Red Feather, the younger brother of Black Shawl, came galloping to Crazy Horse's camp one day with bad news. Woman's Dress, the son of Bad Face, had added another lie to that of Grabber. He had told Three Stars that a scout had listened outside the lodge of Crazy Horse and heard Crazy Horse tell his subchiefs they would take sixty warriors at the coming council and suddenly attack the soldiers, killing all of them. "And," said Red Feather, "there are Indians now planning to come kill you to get favor with White Hat and Three Stars."

Brother Lakotas coming to kill me for the sake of power! he thought. It is indeed as may dream told me. He began planning on how to get Black Shawl to her relatives at the Spotted Tail Agency before he would be ready to die.

Two days later Crazy Horse started for the Spotted Tail Agency with Black Shawl and two warriors, Shell Boy and young Kicking Bear, the brother of Black Fox.

Where now were the clouds of warriors that once had followed the Strange Man into battles at the Rosebud and the Little Bighorn? Instead the little group heard shouting far behind them where No Flesh, with thirty armed Indian Scouts, and No Water with twenty-five more, were hot on their trail, trying no doubt for the reward offered for the death of Crazy Horse. But Crazy Horse still had his canny knowledge of horses and of battle, and he galloped his group down the slopes and walked them up the hills on a route that kept them always ahead of the warriors who followed.

He knew somehow that this was his last time of freedom, and so he drank into his nostrils the keen air of the Moon When the Calves Grow Black Hair, drank into his eyes all the sights of earth and sky, grass flowing away in waves under the wind, the flights of swallows swooping for insects in the swales, the prairie dogs ducking down their den holes as the horses thundered by, and drank in the warm feel of the sun on his skin, and the cool feel of the breeze in his hair. He knew that this freedom was going from his people, but he knew also that in some strange wonderful way it would all come back one day.

In time he saw ahead the tipis of Touch-the-Clouds, his tall cousin of the Minneconjous, and it was Touch-the-Clouds and his warriors who soon rescued him from the pursuing scouts of White Hat, driving them off as the Indians drive the antelope.

When he and Touch-the-Clouds reached the agency of Spotted Tail at Rosebud, the great chief of the Brulés came out with a riding cloud of his warriors, who threatened the Minneconjous until the white officers who were present thought there would surely be war. But Crazy Horse rode between the jeering ranks and lifted his hand in the sign that meant peace, and so sad and troubled was his face that the warriors grew ashamed and were still.

Spotted Tail spoke loudly then about this being his agency and he was in charge if Crazy Horse came there, and Crazy Horse saw that even this great uncle of his, who once had swept a dozen soldiers from their horses in battle, had been forced into guarding his position of leadership, for white and Indian alike were eager to grab it. He had learned to outwit the white agents at their own game and keep his people alive, but his face showed the tension of one who must hold the reins of two mismatched and highly strung horses.

Crazy Horse had not come to make trouble for him, so he just sat quietly until the little soldier chiefs explained that he could not stay at Rosebud but would have to go back to the Crow Butte Agency. But they promised to help him explain to the big soldier chiefs about the lies that had been told about him.

"Let me leave my wife with her people," he asked them, "and let me rest for one night. Then I will go back." Dark was the feeling when he said this, as he knew that at Crow Butte there awaited him nothing but death.

So it was arranged, and he and his wife went to sleep in the lodge of his tall counsin, Touch-the-Clouds, with the excited, anxious voices of his people about him like a flock of frightened birds in a storm cloud.

At first in the morning, riding toward Crow Butte, he was surrounded mainly by friends, such as Touch-the-Clouds, Lieutenant Lee, Bordeaux, a trader, Swift Bear, High Bear, and Black Crow. But soon more and more Brulé scouts in their soldier coats came riding up, and he knew he was a prisoner among his own people. He remembered the great days of old and that last free ride of his, yesterday, through the glory of the fall hills. "They cannot take from me the earth and sky!" he whispered to Touch-the-Clouds.

Near Crow Butte a messenger came, telling Lieutenant Lee to take Crazy Horse to the office of General Bradley, and Crazy Horse felt the noose tightening around him as it does around the rabbit who has tripped the trap on the trail. And only when he looked far away to the edge of the earth could he draw strength from the memory of the days of his youth with Hump, those happy days of the running horses and the good smells of the prairie, and the two great days of his visions, when the Silent One had spoken to him in the voice of the Sparrow Hawk and the voice of the wind in the pines and the cottonwoods.

Now both a good thing and a bad thing happened, one right after the other, like two claps of the thunder. He Dog came galloping up on his bareback horse and reined in beside him to shake his hands with a *"Hou Kola!"* and a straight, warm look that made him a full friend again. But at the fort Little Big Man rushed up not as a friend, but as an enemy, hissing words of hate in his ear and jerking his arm. Yet Crazy Horse was too tired even for shock, and he merely turned and walked into the office where he thought General Bradley was waiting for him, hearing the rising tide of hundreds of voices outside, the sounds full of curiosity and wonder but also with a note of fear as if the Lakotas felt that something bad was going to happen, something they did not want to be affected by because of their fear. And all over the land a darkness was growing, as the night came near, but strangely it was as if a different and terrible darkness were riding in from the east like a great herd of black horses, invisible horses, but permeating the air with sick screams and hate-filled eyes. Crazy Horse looked up suddenly as if he felt their presence, and was searching the darkening sky to see them, but there was only Crow Butte looming to the north and the dull gray streamers of clouds from which the light was fading.

Then he was inside the office and Lieutenant Lee was telling him apologetically that General Bradley had no time to see him now, as it was getting late, but that he would be safe and could go now to rest for the night. There was something twisted about the face of the white officer, as if he were in pain and had been forced to say something he did not believe.

"Hou!" the Indians around Crazy Horse said, and rose to go, but Crazy Horse said nothing, rising as one in a dream to step out into the fading evening, an evening with no color in the sky, but only a dead grayness that had no sense of goodness anywhere, as if somehow earth and sky had forgotten they were once warm and beautiful. And it is often in such a time that the wells of despair and conflict simmering in some men come boiling to the surface in a brief moment of violence to destroy something as wonderful as the rainbow and as fine as the dawn.

Crazy Horse sensed that Little Big Man was part of the permeating sickness that surrounded him, and wondered for a moment why this once strong warrior whom he had trained was now against him. And he sensed also that his few friends who were near were paralyzed into a strange inaction, for none now touched his arm or spoke to him words of encouragement, and he felt as alone as a man would feel who was lost in a vast and hostile sea. But an inner strength made him step firmly forward toward where he was being led.

He walked past a soldier who was walking up

and down with a gun over his shoulder, a gun tipped by a bayonet, and through the open door of a building that was strange to him. Now suddenly he saw the bars in the windows and the men lying against the walls with chains on their legs, and the blood rushed out from his heart in a great wave of anger at this treachery. He turned and as he turned he drew out his knife, the blade flashing in the last light, his whole body violent like that of a mountain lion when the noose falls over its head. But the powerful Little Big Man seized him from behind by both arms, and the two swayed and wrestled like one living creature. Incredible force lashed through his body to drag the much stronger man out the open doorway, while he growled over and over, "Let go of me! Let go of me!" Then with a tremendous jerk he was free, and Little Big Man staggered off with blood running down his arm.

But other Indians seized him now in powerful hands, and the officer of the day was screaming: "Stab him! Kill him! Kill the bastard!"

There was a rending sound behind Crazy Horse, caused by the guard stabbing the door with his bayonet by mistake in his hurry. Then the steel was wrenched out and went plunging into the back of the struggling captive like a lance into the back of a buffalo. There was one more such lunge, the sound of steel in flesh sickeningly soft, and then the voice of Crazy Horse calling quietly, "Let go of me, my friends! You have hurt me enough."

A silence seemed to hang in the air like that which follows a mighty clap of thunder, and the hands that clasped the prisoner dropped from him suddenly so that he staggered and sank to the ground, already covered with his own blood. Where before there had been hate, there was now suddenly a shame and a fear that made many run from the scene with faces blank and staring, their hearts cold and heavy as frozen lead. For both hate and fear had been as heavy in the atmosphere that day as the smoke cloud of terrible fire, and yet somehow now all knew, even the sickest of those present, that a great man was dying because some of them had done nothing to save this Itanca from what others of them did to him.

Crow Butte and the upper White Earth country that surrounded it were soon in darkness while many men thought about that day. Some of Crazy Horse's friends were so wild with grief and anger that others had to restrain them. Some just held their heads in their hands, waiting and waiting, the grief building deep inside. Many remembered now the good and kind things Crazy Horse had done and his great leadership in battle, and numbers thought of his honesty that would not let him compromise with the Wasichus.

He Dog, when allowed to go to the wounded man, put a red blanket over him, and Touch-the-Clouds, alone of all the former friends, had the guts to walk through the ranks of soldiers, like a great ship through the waves, and stand beside his friend, giving up his gun when asked to do so, but saying: ''You are many, I am only one, yet I will trust you!'' shaming the little soldier chief so that he walked away with head bowed.

The angry army doctor came at this time to take charge, furious that nothing had been done by others to stanch the wound and instinctively smelling treachery and rottenness in the whole shoddy affair.

''This is no place for him!'' he roared. ''We must get him moved to a better room, where he can be kept warm.'' So Crazy Horse was moved to the adjutant's office nearby by several strong and gentle hands, moaning and growling at enemies he still felt hovering around him, but gradually quieting under the doctor's sleeping medicine. Here only Touch-the-Clouds was allowed to sit with him. And far away over the land in darkness there seemed to come a soft moaning song, as of many women keening over the death of a beloved. And in that darkness there were some who sought angrily for Little Big Man, remembering the great dream of Crazy Horse that he would be killed only when held by the hands of one of his own, and remembering that other time when Little Big Man had held him when No Water had shot him with his pistol. But Little Big Man was far away by now.

Later that night Worm, the father of Crazy Horse, came like a shadow out of the darkness, his wrinkled face pinched with sorrow, his hand seeking that of his son, and his words calling into the gulf between them: "My son, my son, I am here!" But only the deep breathing answered him, and he had to wait through the long, long hours of that night, hoping for words that never seemed to come.

In the darkness before the dawn Crazy Horse stirred and the father bent forward, hearing a rattle starting in the breathing, seeing the eyes open slowly, at first seeing nothing, then settling on the familiar old face that bent near.

"My son, I—am—here!" the broken words came.

The dying man focused his eyes painfully on that wrinkled, weathered face. Then those eyes filled with a sudden but quickly fading glow and he whispered, "My father. You see I am hurt. Tell my people they can hear my voice no longer."

The father bent still closer, but the wide-open

Taken by a U.S. military officer in 1874, this photo is believed by some—but disputed by others—to be Chief Crazy Horse in full Indian dress.

eyes seemed to be staring sightlessly now, and some of the long brown hair slid gently to the floor till Touch-the-Clouds lifted it with a touch like a mother's, raising it to the dead man's chest. Then the two heads of the living bent lower and the tears fell from their eyes as the springs of the mountains of the west send their waters on their way to the far-off sea. Unashamed tears were these that must flow to join the shining waves of the Great Spirit that wash over the heroes who have died after lives of courage, of dedication, and of love.

Index

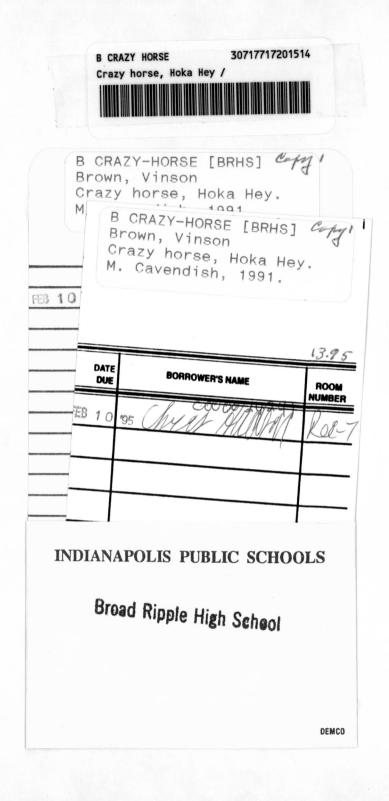

DATE DUE	BORROWER'S NAME	ROOM NUMBER
FEB 10 '95	*Chris Sheldon*	*Rm-7*